Lake Ruth

The Purple and the Gold
THE STORY OF
WESTERN ILLINOIS UNIVERSITY

By Victor Hicken

Western Illinois University Foundation

Macomb, Illinois

Foreword

As Cicero once put it:

> "History is the witness that testifies to the passing
> of time; it illumines reality, vitalizes memory, pro-
> vides guidance in daily life, and brings us tidings
> of antiquity."

In keeping with these ancient and descriptive words, Dr. Victor Hicken, distinguished member of the History faculty of Western Illinois University, has written *The Purple and the Gold*—a warm and masterful review of WIU's past. This history is obviously a labor of devotion, and Dr. Hicken deserves sincere commendation for his generous contribution of time and talent to such an enduring project. The pages that follow contain moments of drama, episodes of mirth, and certainly a veritable flood of glowing memories for Western's sons and daughters. Truly, from *The Purple and the Gold,* comes the strong affection that binds so many to the "College on the Hill."

Today, Western Illinois University is thrusting forward into its dynamic future at an unparalleled rate. No longer a small and placid normal school, it is erupting into public view as a broad-gauged state university with a current enrollment of 11,000 and a projected level of more than 20,000 students by the year 1980. Originally a campus of only 70 acres, W.I.U. now comprises almost 1000 acres—including the Frank J. Horn Field Campus (south of Macomb), and the Kibbe Life Science Station (overlooking the Mississippi, north of Warsaw). Of the total student body, 97% come from various parts of Illinois

(40% from the Chicago metropolitan area alone), and the remaining 3% represent 34 other states and 19 foreign countries. Western's faculty today numbers 575—an outstanding corps of teachers and researchers, 40% of whom hold doctorates, covering the greatly varied activities of seven schools on campus: Applied Sciences, Arts and Sciences, Business, Education, Fine Arts, Graduate Studies, and Health-Physical Education-Recreation. The University presently offers 48 baccalaureates, 32 master's degrees, and one 6th year certificate. Active plans are also being developed for future doctorates in several significant and key areas.

More detail could be added here, but suffice it to say that Western is now engaged in a vigorous—and perhaps arduous!—fulfillment of its historic destiny. In Dr. Hicken's rewarding effort, *The Purple and the Gold*, the seeds of greatness are there for all to peruse. Those of us who are privileged to have a role in Western's mission today are really just agents helping to bring about a phenomenon of unfolding—a fruition of dreams and foundations created long ago.

May all who read these nostalgic pages gain the joy of remembering days of youth and idealism on the campus of Western Illinois University.

John T. Bernhard
President

Macomb, Illinois
February, 1970

Preface

The research which went into the writing of this history of Western Illinois University has taken portions of my time for over the past decade. The first writing was done in 1961; the second in the summer of 1969.

While I was completing the rewrite task this year, it occurred to me that I have spent twenty-two years at Western, and that those years represent almost a third of the history of the school. It has also been revealed to me that I have served under three of Western's six permanent presidents. I was employed during President Beu's tenure of office, and have worked under Presidents Knoblauch and Bernhard. Furthermore, I knew President Morgan well, and had friendly relations with him in the last ten years of his life. I knew a good many faculty members of the Morgan era; many of whom had come to Macomb prior to World War I.

Much of the information about the early years of Western came from these latter people—individuals like Mr. Rupert Simpkins or Mr. George Gaylor. I owe many thanks to men and women who have studied at the school. Mr. James Grigsby gave me much information or told me where to get it, and other alumni wrote letters to me describing events of earlier times. It almost goes without saying that President John T. Bernhard of Western Illinois University has given me much encouragement in putting the history together.

The trouble with doing research so long on a subject, or in being around that subject so long, is that one might write two

histories—one which relates changes as they seem to have occurred—or the other which tells how they actually happened.
All readers will understand that only time allows the second
version in full form. Still, one may recognize here and there a
sprinkling of both; the author's hope being that some future
historian's task may be made easier.

Victor Hicken
Macomb, Illinois
July, 1969

Table of Contents

President John W. Henninger   President Alfred E. Bayliss

The first faculty meeting. Henninger, in middle, is flanked by
Professor Burns, far right, and Professor Fairbank, far left.

President John McGilvrey   President Walter P. Morgan

The Morgan faculty prior to World War II. Morgan is flanked
by Currens on his left, and Simpkins on his right.

President F. A. Beu   President Arthur L. Knoblauch

Veteran's housing—where Corbin Hall now stands. Used during the 1940's and 1950's for married students.

The Beu faculty during World War II.

Sherman Hall prior to World War I. View from the east.

Sherman Hall around 1912. A portion of old athletic field and grandstand can be seen to the left.

The Old Wishing Well—once located near what is now Tillman Hall.

The old library—first floor, Sherman Hall.

Professor Garwood slices the meat for an English Department party.

The old cafeteria—the top floor of what is now Garwood Hall. Dean Currens is stirring his coffee on the right.

The T-formation, circa 1914. Note players without helmets.

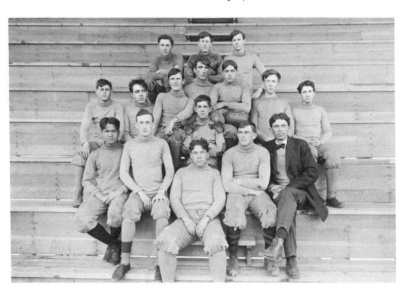

The 1907 football team, which included one Filipino.

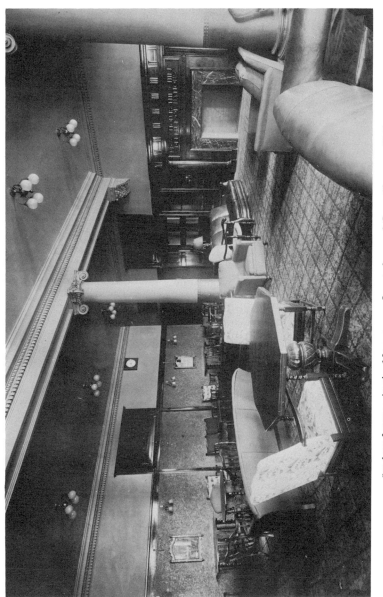

Student Lounge in the Morgan era. Located second floor, Sherman Hall.

With colleagues Garner to his right, and Barclay to his left, "The Rock" rejoins the Marines in World War II.

The "freshman" hockey squad, 1939-1940.

President John T. Bernhard.

A G-I Bill student, circa 1949, hangs up the diapers.

Maxicoats, not in 1970, but in the period before World War I.

Theater in ravine—probably early 1930's.

CHAPTER I

The Beginning

The year was 1900 and the month was December. All over the Christian world the coming of the Yuletide was being heralded; the event being less than one week away.

In Washington, D.C., William McKinley sat in the White House contemplating the end of a term which by all accounts he considered successful. He could not have guessed that he was but a few months away from his death at the hands of an assassin. Rather at this moment he must have sensed the awesome strength of a nation in growth and change. The land was prosperous while at peace. A war had just been won and, though not a big one, it had caused the world to note the emergence of a new power. The American flag, as a consequence, now floated over Yankee garrisons in such far flung places as Manila, Hawaii, Guam, and Puerto Rico.

By the turn of the century the country was truly sectionalized. There was even in the terms of the time, a megalopolitan industrial East, teeming with newly arrived immigrants from Erin, Bohemia, Italy, and Germany. Some levels of society in this section of the nation were wealthy and very, very sophisticated. Other levels, such as those to be found on the East Side of New York City, were crude and very, very poor.

Completely alien to this melting pot of form and humanity was a changing South. Here the remnants of the old Bourbons clashed with and eventually melded with the advance guard of tobacco and industrial interests.

In the West, the old generation of sourdoughs, grubstakers, and cattlemen was passing on. The Indian had found it healthier to live on the reservation rather than off, and a whole breed of optimistic and vibrant Americans had just been born.

One section remained comparatively unchanged from the previous decade, and that was the Middle West. Yet, assumptions could not be freely made about this area of the country. Chicago, for instance, still remained as the most bumptious and aggressive of American cities, even after a brilliant parting goodbye from the British poet, Rudyard Kipling. "Having seen it," he was reputed to have said, "I earnestly desire never to see it again."

Kipling's great mistake was that he had seen only a part of what was truly America. If he had traveled southward, for instance, veering slightly to the west, he would have arrived in the western section of Illinois. Here, two rivers, the Illinois and the Mississippi, form a natural barrier against what some may even today call "foreign influences." In this realm of isolation, both geographical and cultural, was situated a town which might be described by an American "Baedeker" as typically midwestern. Its name is Macomb and it is, to a large extent, the subject of this history.

II.

Though Macomb may have been immune to cosmopolitan doctrines and culture, it was not immune to innovation. The day of December 21 in the last year of the old century, or in the twelfth month of the new, whichever one wishes to call it, proved this to be so. The main square was almost deserted. Indeed, down at Pennebaker's Drug Store, representing the "ultimate" in pharmaceuticals, the clerks must have thought it useless to stay open; business was that slow. Over at Gilfrey's Ice Cream Parlor, Mr. Hendee, the proprietor, did close his shop, for, with the happenings out west of town and the cold of these December days, there was little reason for which to stay open.[1]

There were happenings west of town. Out on the bare edge of settlement where, on a better and warmer day than this, one could stand and see the undulations of the terminal moraines which flank the Mississippi, there was great activity and movement. Children running along the rim of the unfinished street and through the ranks of the hundreds of people watching, were both frightened and delighted by the thunderous blasts of the Hotchkiss gun brought to the parade by the naval reserves from Quincy, sixty miles away. Over on a hill stood a small platform upon which was seated the Governor of the state of Illinois, his head bared to the raw and chilly wind. Down away from the stand, twenty or thirty paces, there was a boy dressed warm to the weather with stocking cap and scarf, living through a moment which was to be one of the most exciting of his long life.

A few years later, Governor John R. Tanner would be dead, and the bunting which had decorated the platform would be dusted and worn, and useless to the touch. The cornerstone laid on that day would become part of a larger structure, beautiful unto itself, but stark looking against the bleak hillside. The boy would grow and mature, and would in time become a proud witness to almost every cornerstone laying on that university campus. There was, indeed, a lesson to be learned on that day —the simple pattern and continuum of life.[2]

III.

It was, in a sense, inevitable that the Western Illinois Normal School would eventually become a fact of history. After 1890 there was a sudden change in the intellectual atmosphere of the nation. It was almost like a breath of fresh air which swept over the campuses of the country's universities. One noted historian describes it as a craving for knowledge which resulted in widening sale of books, the almost wild popularity of literary magazines, and a great rush by young men and women to the universities and normal schools, eager in search of an education. Throughout the land, colleges and normal schools blossomed into being at a frightening rate. In many of them the buildings were hastily and poorly constructed, and the faculties were both poorly chosen and paid. Others of them had more auspicious starts, however. In these, the buildings had some degree of permanence and the faculties were peopled with brilliant young scholars who, according to one American historian, were desirous of replacing "American superficiality with the Teutonic idea of patient thoroughness."[3]

By the middle of the 1890's, the new craze for normal schools had reached Illinois. The state already had one such institution located near Bloomington and called the Illinois State Normal School. Established in 1857, the "Old Normal" had achieved a fine reputation by the turn of the century. So successful had it been that in 1869 the State Legislature passed a bill which created the Southern Illinois Normal School.

The "nineties" really saw an atmosphere conducive to normal school growth. Normal schools were chartered for DeKalb and Charleston, principally as a result of sectional political forces operating in the northern and eastern areas of the state. Shortly thereafter, in the same kind of spirit, the politicians and businessmen of Western Illinois pressed for the creation of a similar school in that part of the state.

IV.

A very wise citizen of Macomb once said that it was ridiculous to assume that politics as a practice and as an influence had no place on a college campus. Political spoils, so said the same writer, had led to the very notion of a Western Illinois Normal School. The institution, he concluded, was "conceived in politics," and "born in political strife."[4]

This was in every syllable and word a true statement. Early and late in the midsummer evenings of 1899 the gas lights of the period flickered for long hours in the law offices surrounding the Macomb city square. One might suppose that the same activity was going on elsewhere in Western Illinois, though not with quite the same urgency of purpose.

A group of men were at work framing a bill: a bill so drawn and written that it would be difficult to locate the state normal planned for the western part of the state in any town other than Macomb. One of the gentlemen, Lawrence Y. Sherman, was so influential a politician that one day in the future he would be seriously considered for the presidential nomination at a Republican National Convention. Sherman was a tall, slender, and politically oriented man who had, in the manner of Lincoln, ridden pennilessly into Macomb a few years before. Now in 1899, he was not only Macomb's most successful lawyer, but was Speaker of the Illinois House of Representatives as well.[5]

As the bill was drawn, Sherman's ideas came to pervade it, and his energy gave impetus to it. He persuaded a Representative Black of Schuyler County to introduce the measure, since as Speaker he could not be expected to do so. The bill was handily passed, as one might suspect with such strength behind it, and forwarded to Governor Tanner for his signature. It is a further credit to Sherman and a mere indication of his political strength to note that, when Tanner vetoed the new normal school bill, it took relatively few words from the Macomb politician whispered discreetly in the Governor's ear to cause Tanner to change his mind. And that, one may add, was just about how it was between Sherman and the Governor until the latter died.[6]

So the bill became law on April 24, 1899. Since it did not specifically state the location of the school, Governor Tanner almost immediately appointed a committee of leading citizens in Western Illinois for the purpose of locating the new institution within the regulations set forth in the original act. It may be assumed that Sherman gave Tanner considerable guidance in the choice of the Board of Trustees designated to place and administer the school. They were tactfully chosen from the area about Macomb in such a way that, if one were to locate the home towns of each upon a map of Western Illinois by pins, he would be struck by the similarity to a pinwheel with Macomb as hub.

With the exception of two of the members of this original Board of Trustees there is little reason to recount their names. John Keefer of Macomb, both at this point of the story and later, would play an important role in the development of Western, as would Alfred Bayliss who, in 1899, was the State Superintendent of Public Instruction.

The first meeting of the trustees, held in Bushnell, Illinois, was brief, practical, and businesslike. The gentleman from Monmouth was elected temporary president, and John Keefer from Macomb became the acting secretary. The Board was scheduled to meet next at Galesburg on August 31, and would accept at that time all formal applications from any city interested in having the new normal located within its corporation. The only stipulation by the Board was that each site should be larger than thirty acres.

The happenings between July 20, the date of the first meeting, and August 14 were quite significant, and presented a turn of events entirely unexpected by those in Macomb who had formulated such well laid plans. By August 2, Keefer had on record nominations from Monmouth, Oquawka, Aledo, La-Harpe, Rushville, and Quincy, as well as Macomb.

Even at this point, however, confidence reigned on the main square between Lafayette and Randolph streets in the latter town. It was true that rumors were rife that Macomb was to have competition in the fight for the school, but didn't this

city have Speaker Sherman on its side? It was a confidence
scarcely dented by news notes of the strenuous efforts which
each of the nominated towns was exerting toward acquiring the
school. As one contemporary described those efforts:

> Never did these towns present such a beautiful appearance. Streets
> were swept, weeds were cut, trash was burned, fences were white-
> washed, stagnant pools were skimmed and fresh water pumped in,
> children's faces were washed, Sunday clothes were put on. In some
> cases it is said blankets were spread over the graveyards.[7]

The real shocker to the Macomb politicians came with the
news of the various bids which the other towns had managed to
scrape together. Rushville, for example, gathered together pledg-
es of $120,000 with other considerations as its offer to the
Board. It was even rumored in Macomb that every taxpayer in
Rushville had placed himself under obligation to contribute.
Monmouth offered $54,000 as an inducement to the Board,
LaHarpe presented the sum of $10,000, and Quincy came up
with $30,000. Since Macomb offered only $70,000 and a site,
one can understand the sudden fear on the part of various citizens that the school would go elsewhere.

After preliminary meetings in which each town presented
its propositions to the Board, the trustees began serious balloting on the location of the school on September 1. From this
point on, and for the next several weeks, the contest waxed hot
and heavy. The initial advantage which Macomb assumed it
had in the writing of the bill seemed to vanish. As it should
have been supposed in the beginning, each member of the
Board supported his own favorite town; and only in Keefer's
case was it Macomb.[8]

Once again, this was a tremendous disappointment to the
Macomb group, for they had assumed that only one balloting by
the Board would determine their city to be the site for the new
normal. It was reputed that when Keefer saw the results of the

first vote which showed an almost even distribution of choices made by Board members, he was astonished. "Why, I thought you fellows knew the school was to go to Macomb," he reportedly said.[9]

All through the month of September in 1899 the Board balloted, with scarcely any change in the nature of the voting. On November 7, in an executive session, it voted one hundred and twelve times without coming to a decision. By the end of sixty-one separate sessions held by the group, the number of individual ballots taken by the members amounted to five hundred and ninety-seven. In view of the fact that each balloting must have been tension ridden to some degree, it is understandable that the patience of all concerned with the problem of locating the school came to a state of exhaustion.

V.

The *Historical Encyclopedia of Illinois,* as published at the turn of the century, describes Macomb in simple and direct terms. It was, the article states, the county seat of McDonough County; having some 5,375 people, a thriving sewer-pipe factory, a drain-tile works, a pottery plant, and a school-desk casting firm. Furthermore, concludes the description, it was the location of an interurban electric car line; the Chicago, Burlington, and Quincy railroad; various banks and schools, four newspapers; and assorted business establishments.[11]

In all actuality, Macomb in 1900 was a little more than the brief description implies. Any settlement cannot be crystallized into perspective of time and place by the mere facts of an encyclopedia. In order to achieve this, one must put the town into its proper setting, and hold them both at some distance in order to catch the refraction of times past and present.

A noted night club comedian once said of Western Illinois that "things get so quiet in the summer . . . that the Mississippi River runs only three times a week." To one looking at the area from the urban point of view, there is some truth in this. There are parts of Western Illinois, Pike or Calhoun counties, for example, in which even today time never seems to move. The villages are still perched on the same hills, or in the small valleys, as they were a hundred years ago. The tempo of life is still slow, and one may hear the ancient phrases and old words which John Hay used in his *Pike County Ballads* nearly a century ago. Indeed, one may even hear them in Macomb on Saturday night, for many farmers still come into town to shop then, or on Friday nights when the stores stay open extra late. The old tendencies are still there—the strengthening of weak verbs, the weakening of strong ones, the use of verbs as nouns, and the wild experimentation with the English language which was so common on the frontier years ago. It is not unusual, therefore, to hear "clumb" for climbed, "growed" for grew, and "throwed" for threw. Nor is it uncommon to note the use of the verb "invite" for invitation.

This is not to ridicule such speech, for it is indeed as colorful as it is broad, and it is typical of the background and origins of the people themselves. They are the products of a frontier ancestry which brought such usages to Illinois over a hundred years ago. Particularly did these early settlers come from Tennessee and Kentucky, settling to the south of a line running from east to west and just north of Macomb. These people came up through the southern part of the state after the War of 1812, riding their "Tennessee" wagons on which was loaded everything they owned, in search of land in the newly opened Military tract. The latter title was given to that area between the Illinois and Mississippi rivers which was to be distributed by the federal government to the veterans of the recent war in the form of land bonuses. Thus, for the thirty years following the War of 1812 such immigrants filled up the land from Pike County in the south, through McDonough in the middle, to Rock Island County in the north. They named their settlements after heroic admirals or generals of the conflict just finished, or of the revolutionary period. On occasion, as in the case of Industry or Good Hope, they chose the virtues; in other instances the towns were simply named after the principal founders.

After 1850, a change in the pattern of immigration began to take place. Great numbers of New England Yankees, fleeing their poor farms in Massachusetts or New Hampshire, came to Illinois in search of what the land advertisements called the good life. Many of them found a version of it in the Military Tract north of Macomb, and in such cities as Galesburg and Farmington. It is, indeed, no coincidence that the town of Macomb, right on the dividing line between two ways of life, would have on one side of it the village of Vermont, and on the other the village of Tennessee.

By the late 1850's new immigrant groups began to take their places in the Military Tract. Swedes, coming for both political and religious reasons, settled in the region about Galesburg and Rock Island; and Germans, emigrating for reasons of military conscription in the German states, the desire for political freedom, and the failure of crops in that part of Europe, settled in the section about Moline and Rock Island. Both groups were readily assimilated into the prosperous agrarian economy of Western Illinois.

It may be said with some truth that each group added its own particular mortar to the solid conservative philosophy which exists in the Military Tract. The southerners who came first were never truly aligned Jacksonian Democrats. They were, as described by many early politicians, very conservative Clay Whigs, sold on the virtue of tradition and weak federal power. Even Lincoln had great difficulty in raising votes in McDonough County, the heart of the Military Tract. As far as can be ascertained, he never carried McDonough in the three elections in which the citizens of that county had the opportunity to vote for him. Even in the election of 1864, at the height of the great war, the voters of McDonough cast their lot with McClellan as opposed to Lincoln. The fact of the matter was that, in each of the three elections, Lincoln appeared as the liberal candidate.

The Yankees, Swedes, and Germans settling in the Military Tract tended to align themselves with the new Republican Party after 1865. They still tend to vote for the "grand old party," except when divided by local issues or religious ties. In a sense, it is as described by one indignant Democrat of southern Illinois not so long ago—"Why up in that area, they hunt Democrats with shotguns."

If one were to describe Macomb today, he would have to state frankly that fundamentally it hasn't changed much in the seventy years. It is still cut in half by the Chicago, Burlington, and Quincy railroad; it still has its pottery and porcelain works, and it is still a city directed by agrarian and small business interests.

To be sure, it has almost four times the population as it had some seventy years ago, but one must hasten to point out that much of the area surrounding it has declined substantially in density. It is still a delightful town in which to live, were one to except the miserable months of January and February when the whole area appears to be one of muddy snow and frozen mud, and when the only thing in full bloom is the sinus complaint. So it is, that the one essential difference wrought in the town over the seventy year span has been in the appearance of Western Illinois University.

VI.

Some attempt has been made here to indicate the sudden shock which struck the citizens of Macomb when they found that, despite the contents of the normal school bill as framed by Sherman, it appeared as if the proposed school would be located somewhere else. Many of the local politicos felt that the other towns were in the way of conspiring together to deprive Macomb of the project, particularly after the balloting continued on and on without decision. In a sense this was true; for by Christmas time of 1899 three of the other towns had built up enough support to stand the chance of winning the prize. These were Aledo, Monmouth, and Rushville. The next meeting, the one following the holidays, would determine the winner, for one absentee member of the Board would return to the meetings, and he had been pledged to vote for one of the three.

For Macomb this was the point of desperation. Here, however, the fine political hand of Sherman again showed itself. There may have been hurried consultations in Springfield with the Governor, or there may have been messages sent by wire, but whatever the method the next event was a shocker. Since the Macomb cause could not afford another ballot with the existing Board of Trustees, the only resort was to abolish this group and to appoint a new one. This Governor Tanner did.[12]

The new Board, chosen from all parts of the State and theoretically less liable to political pressures of a local nature, met in August of 1900 for the first time. Once again, days and weeks were taken to inspect the proposed sites, and to listen to new propositions. Macomb, this time, raised its offer to $70,000 in cash, a thirty acre site, the promise of pavement to the location, adequate sewerage facilities, electric lights, gas, and water free for ninety-nine years. It also added as a bonus the free use of the new Carnegie library. This time Sherman appeared in person to lead the fight for the Macomb group. Armed with a wooden map so constructed that a plumb held from any part of it would point to Macomb, and with powerful arguments that Macomb was the logical location for the school in the frame of reference designated by the bill, the Board was quickly swayed.

It is almost impossible to overestimate the influence which Sherman had with the new Board. On the first ballot, conducted

in the Leland Hotel in Springfield, August 14, Macomb was ad-
judged to be the winner of the new proposed normal school. A
happy Macomb delegation ran to the telegraph office in order
to wire to the *Macomb Journal* reporter then waiting in the
local railroad station. "Macomb won on the first ballot," read
the message. There was little sleep in the town that night, for
the bells rang late, and the happy celebrators exploded cannon
into the hours of the morning.[13]

VII.

Not unexpectedly, the public reaction of the surrounding
areas to the choice of Macomb was a highly unfavorable one.
Disappointed towns refused to accept the Governor's explanation that he had chosen the new Board simply because the old
one hadn't done the task asked of it by the legislature. Any
suggestion from the same source that the new group was filled
with men of "integrity, ability, and sagacity" passed over those
who had sought the prize and lost. Any proposition that the
Governor merely wanted the best location was hooted and
ridiculed. Looking at the uproar from the distance of seventy
years, one quickly arrives at the conclusion that the rejected
towns were not so much angry at having lost as at the manner by
which they were defeated. The *Rock Island Argus*, speaking for
these towns in general, stated that the first Board "did not hold
any promising prospect for Speaker Sherman's home town...."
"More care was taken in the selection of the new board," it
continued, "and Macomb got the school on the first ballot."

The people of Aledo were particularly angry at the result of
the new Board's action. They had come startlingly close to final
victory in the sessions of the earlier group, and were bitter at
the turn of events. "Misery loves company...," wrote a Monmouth paper, "and dear Miss Aledo, we tip our hat to you in
your sad hour of bereavement." One gathers that the inhabitants
of this pretty little town were close to some kind of violent ac-

tion over the manner in which the decision was made. There was, at least, considerable talk on the Aledo main street about the possibility of "bribery" in the giving of the victory to Macomb.

There was no joy in Quincy, either. This city, which saw in Macomb a strong rival to its preeminent economic position in Western Illinois, had fought the winning town tooth and nail for the school. Perhaps the most bitter charges made in the fight came from the Quincy and Macomb factions. The Macomb group raised the issue of Quincy's water supply, charging that it was bad and unhealthful. Quincy quickly retaliated by claiming that Macomb had four hundred water taps, but the city water was so impure that only two hundred families used the supply. Now that the school had been won by Macomb, the implications and imprecations made during the fight could now be forgotten by the people of the winning town, but not by those of Quincy. The *Quincy Herald* said that the whole situation surrounding the location of the normal was rife with politics. If Sherman had "been a citizen of Goose Island, the stately walls of the normal would have risen on Goose Island," the paper concluded.

There were other reactions. The *Henderson County Democrat* argued that the decision was simply a piece of "political jobbery." The *Aledo Democrat* could not leave the thing alone, pointing out that there would still be other elections in the future to be decided, and the citizens of Western Illinois might make their feelings show at the polls. "If the trustees were not fixed for Macomb," it stated, "they fixed themselves good and plenty." The *Carthage Republican*, thinking of the future of the private college located in that town, argued that there was no need for a normal school anyway, and that the politicians had really determined the existence of the new school. The *Chicago Tribune*, speaking from some distance as the voice of Illinois Republicanism, confirmed Sherman's role in the fight. It was very simply a personal victory for the Illinois politician, the paper stated.[14]

In Macomb the feeling was one of satisfaction and elation. Now there was time for philosophical recollection as to how it had all been accomplished, and who was really responsible for the victory. John Keefer, whose term on the first board had been a frustrating one, gave the credit for the whole idea to Jacob C. Thompson who was, at that time, studying law in the Macomb office of L. Y. Sherman. Thompson, said Keefer, not only got the inspiration for the school, but did Sherman's leg work in compiling the information for the legislation which did the job. Sherman, on the other hand, gave full credit to C. V. Chandler, Albert Eads, and W. H. Hainline, all local citizens who had taken part in the fray. For what it all meant, however, there was really enough credit for all.[15]

VIII.

Among the instructions set out by the second Board of Trustees concerning the actual location of the school were the following regulations. It must be placed upon a "suitable site of from twenty to sixty acres," said the flyer. It must have a good water supply and be located in a healthful and properly drained area, and it must be connected to the "main portion" of the town by road and sidewalk.[16]

It would seem passing strange that, after such a great struggle to obtain the new state normal, there would follow a short but spirited fight as to where within Macomb it should be built. Even today, when one looks at Macomb in an objective manner, it is impossible to find a better location for the school than that upon which it was constructed. Yet, there was a quarrel. The "Wheat" site, that upon which the school eventually rose, was condemned by many because they felt that the land was too rolling, that the barren clay hill "unsoftened by ... shrubbery and trees" was too ugly, and that an exbrickyard (which had actually existed upon the spot) was esthetically speaking no place upon which to build an exalted edifice.[17]

The Board was in no mood to prolong the problem which had given them so much grief, however. All through the summer of 1900 the trustees pushed forward the plan to construct on the "Wheat" site, and prodded the city of Macomb on its unfulfilled obligations. It was in November that construction was started on the new building with Jacob C. Thompson ceremoniously expropriating the spade used to turn the first piece of sod.[18]

IX.

The building of the school now under way, the Board turned toward the task of acquiring a faculty. The initial step here would be, of necessity, the employment of the first principal or president of the institution. One must use the latter terms interchangeably, for though the word principal was in common use for educational administrators of normal schools at that time, one finds the trustees of such institutions referring to the same office with the alternate title. Though it wasn't until the coming of Walter Piety Morgan to the presidency in 1912 that the term principal was finally dropped, hereinafter the word president will be used.

There were a number of applicants for the presidency, quite naturally. Late in 1901, the Board established the broad principles under which the new appointment would act; a frame of reference which has, to a large extent, been applicable since that time. The president would insure "efficiency in all of the departments," keep a "constant watch and care over every school interest" as well as instructional work, select "competent and right-spirited" faculty members. In return, the Board would expect the president to "act with perfect freedom within the lines of general policy laid down by the Board."[19]

What the Board did not state, however, but what was certainly true with regard to state colleges of that time, was that politics would to a large extent rule the makeup of the first Western faculty—from the president to its lowest member. More will be written on the subject later, but this much can be pointed out here—the choice of Western's first president (as well as some of the later ones) was politically motivated, and the choice of Western's first faculty was made partially upon the basis of political expediency. The last was motivated principally by the desire to heal the wounds caused by the selection of Macomb as the location of the normal, many of the faculty being hired from neighboring towns. The story as to how John Wesley Henninger became Western's first president becomes a little more involved, however.[20]

If one could shatter the facade of time, and get at the proper picture of events as they occurred in 1901, it would probably show that two individuals actually wanted the appointment to the presidency of the school. It can be said, strangely enough, that both men actually obtained the position, but not at the same time or under the same circumstances.

By the fall of 1901, the whole political situation in the state had changed from that happy state of affairs which existed the year before. Tanner was gone, and in his place was Governor Richard Yates. Though both the former governor and his successor were of the same Republican persuasion, each represented a different faction within the party. Tanner had received considerable support from Sherman, while Sherman in turn had reaped a large share of the political spoils of Tanner's administration. Sherman was not a Yates man, however, and never would be. Consequently, the Macomb politician could not expect or receive favors from the new Governor.

As it developed, both Sherman and Yates had their own candidates for the position of the presidency of Western Illinois State Normal School. John W. Henninger, from the home town of the new governor, Jacksonville, was the choice of Yates, and one can see at this point that the state executive's opinion eventually prevailed. Alfred E. Bayliss, the State Superintendent of Public Instruction and a member of the Western Board of Trustees by virtue of his office, also wished for the president's position and had Sherman's support for the post. Henninger, one must hasten to add, likewise held a position in the state administration. Paradoxically, he was Bayliss's aide, the Assistant Superintendent of Public Instruction.

Once more there was another short but bitter political fight. Again, it might be stated that politics as a practice was part and parcel of state supported education at the turn of the century. Bayliss used his position within the Board to oppose Henninger's appointment, voting instead for Charles McMurry, a famous proponent of normal school education then living in DeKalb, Illinois. McMurry would hardly have taken the post, he was becoming that well known nationally, and it appears that Bayliss was perversely throwing his vote to an unwilling candidate.

In October Henninger won the position outright, with Bayliss voting against him down to the final wire. As long as Henninger held the presidency, which would be until the state political picture changed, he and Bayliss continued to be political opponents, friendly only in official relationships which they had to have. When the political situation evolved, when Yates was supplanted with a pro-Bayliss and Sherman governor, Henninger was promptly replaced in the presidency by his old opponent, Alfred E. Bayliss.[21]

X.

Henninger held the presidency for almost four years. Leaving character and personal description to another time and place, it might be appropriate to insert at this point some details of his life. They are only vague details at that, for of all of Western's presidents he is the hardest to pin down, the most ephemeral in terms of facts. Two are certain, however, and they

are that Henninger was primarily a Methodist minister, and
secondly a politician. He was born at Hagerstown, Illinois, a
town no longer appearing on state maps, in the year of 1857. He
would have been approximately forty-four years of age when
assuming the presidency of Western, a comparatively young
man for such a position. He died in 1918 in Bloomington, Illinois, probably in the Spanish influenza epidemic. He finished a
degree at McKendree College in Lebanon, Illinois, in 1881,
teaching thereafter in a number of places including Vandalia
and Mt. Carmel. Meanwhile, he continued to complete graduate
work at the University of Chicago, receiving a Master of Arts
degree in 1907, two years after leaving the presidency of Western. His remaining years were spent in holding a position at
Illinois Wesleyan University, where he taught political science.
At the high point of his career he appears as a vigorous man,
mustachioed and dark, quite handsome, and addicted to fine
horses. Now, in 1901, however, what he would say and do would
profoundly affect the future of the newest of the Illinois normal
schools.[22]

Notes to Chapter I: *A Beginning*

1. *Macomb Bystander,* July 31, 1901. This issue was entirely devoted to business
growth of the town. It points out that the city was noted for sewerpipe and
stoneware industries, the location of Phelps Hospital which was equipped for
the "scientific treatment of disease," brick works, soft drink plants, and cigar
making facilities.

2. *Macomb Journal,* Dec. 27, 1900. The *Journal* noted: "While the day dawned
auspiciously for the exercises, yet clouds soon filled the sky, obscuring the sun,
and the south wind which blew steadily all day made the atmosphere raw and
chilly." Tanner gave a long address, stressing the fact that "the republic will
need the services of these boys and girls in some critical time to come." After
the cornerstone laying, a dinner was given for Tanner. Attendance was by
special invitation, and a meal consisting of turkey, scalloped oysters, boiled ham,
chicken salad, ice cream, and salted almonds was served by the Hotel Newcomb,
Quincy. By the way, the little boy might have been Wayne Wetzel, who has attended nearly every cornerstone laying on the Western campus.

3. Arthur Schlesinger, Sr., *The Rise of the City,* p. 211. Oliver M. Dickerson,
in his letter of February, 1961, to the author, claims that there was a revolution
in classroom methodology and curriculum, that students were in a state of
revolt against "overemphasis upon method" in the teachers colleges.

4. *Macomb Journal,* June 20, 1942.

5. Interview with Mrs. Leroy Stocker, Macomb, Illinois. Mrs. Stocker is the daughter of John Keefer, Macomb's first Board member, and is the "Ruth" after whom Lake Ruth is named.

6. One is reminded of the famous humorist "Mr. Dooley," and his description of Theodore Roosevelt who appointed a committee to investigate a phase of activities, and ordered it to make sure that the final report substantiated his own prejudices upon the subject.

7. Newton Bateman and Paul Selby, *Historical Encyclopedia of McDonough County,* p. 696.

8. *Sequel,* 1934.

9. *Quincy Herald,* n.d.; this was a clipping forwarded to writer by Mrs. J. B. Glasgow, the daughter of James Burns, Western's first history professor.

10. *Minutes of the Board of Trustees,* 1899. These are now in the possession of the Vice President for Business Affairs of Western Illinois University.

11. Bateman and Selby, *op. cit.,* p. 348.

12. *Macomb Journal,* June 20, 1942, October 22, 1949.

13. *Ibid.,* Sept. 25, 1902. The fact that the *Journal* had a man waiting in the telegraph office would indicate confidence in Sherman. It is reputed that the wooden map used by Sherman is still in the Macomb area.

14. All clippings forwarded by Mrs. J. B. Glasgow. Strong words such as "bribery" and "fixed" were used in relation to the decision.

15. Mrs. Stocker gives much credit to Thompson; so does *Sequel,* 1934.

16. *Regulations for Establishment of Western Illinois Normal School,* a pamphlet issued by the Board of Trustees, 1900. Now in possession of Vice President for Business Affairs, W. I. U.

17. *Western Courier,* June 8, 1921. Also *Sequel,* 1934.

18. *Sequel,* 1934. Spade now in Office of the President, W. I. U.

19. *Minutes of the Board of Trustees,* 1901.

20. Dickerson to this writer, February, 1961. Schlesinger in *The Rise of the City* points out that the influence of politics in colleges was great. He states that the whole faculty of Kansas Agricultural College was dismissed in 1897 for subscribing to Populist beliefs. Another fine treatment of the same subject is given in Charles Harper's *A Century of Public Teacher Education,* 1939.

21. *Monmouth Review,* a clipping from the Glasgow collection. One can see the fight developing in *Board of Trustee's Minutes,* 1901. The McMurry referred to is Charles Alexander McMurry, a professor of methodology at Northern Illinois Normal. McMurry was one of those scholars profoundly influenced by study in Germany.

22. *Courier,* Dec. 6, 1918.

CHAPTER II

The Henninger Era

Ten years after the opening of the doors of the Western Illinois State Normal School, Miss Caroline Grote, much beloved among the student body then and later, described what is now Sherman Hall as a "magnificent classic structure of stone and marble, combining size, massive strength, and classic beauty. . ." In that year, 1911, the first floor of the building was given over to the training school for novitiate teachers, to domestic science, and to the domestic arts. The second floor had a study hall, the various laboratories necessary to a school of this type, a book and supply store, the library, and administrative offices. The third floor contained the auditorium, recitation rooms, art and music rooms, and meeting halls for various student societies.[1]

One may note that the above is the description of a finished building organized to the complexity of dealing with an increasing student body. Actually, what existed at this point in the history of the institution was the end product of great effort on the part of the college Board, and countless headaches suffered by two separate and distinct administrations. What ought to be written here is that during the Henninger period, and in the Bayliss era which followed, the first building was in the process of gradual and painfully slow construction. Perhaps it also needs to be added that what resulted from all of this effort is still the most solid and orthodox of the college's buildings, and further still, one which may exist as such for some decades to come.

21

Those problems in the construction and staffing of the building which were President Henninger's primarily, and the Board's secondarily, seemed almost monumental and insurmountable in the early days and months of the institution. There were, in fact, few paved roads in Macomb, and none to the location of the school proper. One contemporary of the period describes "main street" of Macomb as an unpaved no-man's land of mud and horse rails.[2] After the flush of victory in the school fight had died away, the town found itself with the task of undertaking the laying of pavement from the main section to the new campus. In one grand gesture of munificence, with undoubtedly a few afterthoughts, the city administration proceeded to pave not only the route from the business section through Adams Street and to the school, but the main square as well.[3] One may conjecture that the town's magnificent extravagance must have overwhelmed many a student from less fortunate villages in the years to come. The same student would still have familiar conditions with which to cope: the outdoor "Chic Sales," or the open sewage ditches running through the town.

Though Adams Street would eventually seem to be a splendid thoroughfare, roads running from that avenue through the campus would be slow in coming. The initial road, that which still swings in front of old Sherman Hall from and back to Adams, existed as a wagon path for some time even after the building was finished. Later it would be filled with broken tile and debris from the local sewerpipe factory; a condition which would last until around 1907. There were no sidewalks in the beginning, and there would be none for some time to come. The first students of the Normal were forced to pick their way across open fields, or over plank walks laid for their convenience, in order to arrive at classes.[4]

As has been pointed out, Sherman Hall was, and still is, a grand and imposing structure. When one considers the great strain endured by all in its construction, the conclusion that it ought to have been is inevitably reached. The initial work was done in November of 1900 when heavy concrete footings consisting of locally supplied sand and crushed stone from northern Illinois were laid. The walls of the foundation, those seen by venturesome students who pass through the tunnel between Simpkins Hall and Sherman Hall today, were built of Naperville stone, with each piece firmly and laboriously laid in place.

The work seemed to go slowly then and even more so from the vantage of seventy years time, especially when one notes the rapid manipulation of beam and stone into dormitories and classroom buildings in the 1970's. In 1900, however, much of the work had to be done by hand and muscle. The heavy grey canon stone from Ohio was placed in position over the foundation by large and cumbersome wooden cantilevers or scaffolds and then lowered. All was finely done, and with the ensuing decades which have passed since the initial work, the main building or Sherman Hall still weathers time more gracefully than many of the newer buildings now surrounding it.[5]

The inside of the building was not finished for some years following the opening of the school. Being some three hundred and twenty feet long, and eighty-six deep, and having a Board of Trustees and an administration anxious to make it a showplace normal school for the entire Midwest, the structure endured agonies of painstaking effort before its final completion. Maple floors were laid over concrete (now the maple is overlaid with various forms of tile), and the vestibules were lined with Italian marble. The walls were elaborately decorated with Victorian rococo, and paneled in spots with darkly stained woods. Illumination was provided with equally elaborate combination gas and electric chandeliers which put forth a dependable, if unsteady, light.[6]

The gymnasium, to be located in what is at this writing an entire complex of administrative offices, was not finished for some time. When completed, its ceiling was raised slightly above the first floor level, allowing for only low trajectory shots at the basketball backboards. Straight above the gymnasium and on the third floor was the auditorium, a room generally considered a splendid prototype for its time. This large enclosure was decorated by four rather large (and some said poorly done) paintings by a Mr. Connors. Another artistic flourish was added by a certain Mr. Holt; obviously a craftsman of considerable talent for his time. Holt did much of the elaborate configuration about the stage, rather romantically placing over the spot "a medallion, containing the likeness of his daughter."[7]

To hundreds of Western students through the years, the auditorium became the most familiar room on the campus. Here the whole student body and faculty met in chapel exercises several times a week, and here the student was given a taste of culture, albeit at times crude and unpolished, but not yet to be found in the hamlets of Schuyler or Pike. Romance and sentiment aside, however, the auditorium was never satisfactory for the type of presentation for which it was designed. The stage was too small, the apparatus too cumbersome, and the accoustics unbelievable. Charles Coburn, famous in the theater for decades, paid two visits to the school in his lifetime. On the occasion of his second visit, which was after World War II and following his first by some thirty-five years, he was heard to remark that the room was one place he had not forgotten in his years on the stage. It was just as unsatisfactory on the second occasion as on the first, he concluded.[8]

It might be well at this point to describe Sherman Hall in general as it appears today. Time has had its way, of course, and the richly burnished woods have given way to tile and paint, a change which most old timers would emphatically agree is no improvement. The main structure is there, nevertheless; and in many cases, rooms which were designed for a particular function still suffice for the same kind of purpose. This is especially true of administrative offices. Yet, changes of a significant nature have occurred. The laboratories, which students will remember for the emittance of foul and unrelenting odors, are now in buildings designed for their noisome nature. The domestic sciences have moved, and so have the physical activities, of course. The library, for years so handy and yet so ridiculously placed, has already found a new home in a tasteful but functionally inappropriate building of its own.

There are those who would claim that buildings have a personality of their own. If true, it would seem that old Sherman has a kind of contradictive dignity to it. This is not of a nature created by whimsical administration which would later paint a social science room a most outrageous shade of pink, or would place a dean of personnel services next to the ladies rest room. It is, instead, a built-in, benign, and perverse kind of dignity which one might find in any seventy year old veteran of strife and struggle. Students and visitors seldom whisper in Sherman Hall, as they might in Tillman Hall or even in the domestic science rooms. On the contrary, it can be suspected that they have the impulse to hail their comrades, or laugh spontaneously over some youthful folly. Perhaps that is the way the building was meant to be in the beginning. Change may seem final to some, and inevitable to all; but there are few, both of old and late comers to the campus, who have really wished youth and Sherman Hall to separate.

II.

As discussed sometime earlier, American education in 1899 and 1900 was in a state of ferment and change. Normal schools were springing up all over the land, new ideas and innovations were being introduced into the curriculum, and there was a great improvement in textbooks during this marked revolution. Charles DeGarmo's *Essentials of Method,* published in 1899, and Charles Alexander McMurry's *General Method,* published in 1892, did much to drive out the old system of drill and rote, and to substitute Herbartianism as a popular educational philosophy.[9]

Herbartianism came into full flood at the turn of the century. Both DeGarmo and McMurry, products of Illinois State Normal, led the fight to spread its doctrines. Since McMurry taught for some time in DeKalb, one can imagine the impact of the new philosophy upon Western Illinois Normal, which opened its door in 1902. As described by one writer, Herbartianism was a "... direct attack upon an entrenched system of method and subject matter in the public schools. It preached the doctrine of interest, the organization of subject matter around fundamental meanings, and the inclusion of vital materials in the curriculum."[10]

Though American education was in a state of flux at the turn of the century, one may suppose that not all of the faculties of the universities of the nation were affected by the change. One writer describes normal school faculties of the time as "uneven" in quality, with many of the people being trained at other teachers colleges, or being taken from the administrative staffs of large high schools. Some such normal instructors were only "certificated" individuals, having indicated some mastery of subject matter with a bare knowledge of pedogogical principles.

In each normal school the most significant individual was the president. Facilities of such schools were small, and individual members, having little recourse to faculty government, were weak in personal power. Hence, the school was what the president made of it. He was generally the registrar, the curriculum specialist, the publicity agent, the employer, and he taught a schedule of classes as well. He often carried an academic title, and he occasionally supervised student teaching or acted as head of the training school.

Presidents of this time were chosen on the basis of sheer power of personality. They were often dynamos of energy with a great sense of duty and responsibility. They considered it very important to impress their students with the same concept of life, and one comes to the conclusion that their only educational goal was to turn out "good" and hard working graduates. They chose their faculties by the same rule. Faculties, too, must be energetic and well known. "The presidents of the normals," says one writer, "were as a rule keenly aware *that the school was the faculty.*"[11] It may be seen that Western fitted the national pattern.

III.

In the late April days of 1902, the newly appointed faculty members of Western Illinois Normal began to arrive in the city of Macomb. President Henninger called them into faculty session at the Hotel Chandler (near the park of that name), and soon the machinery of faculty business began to move. Committees were appointed to deal with courses of study, athletics, literary societies, "Christian Work," and other activities. Textbooks were to be chosen, advertising for students was to be written, various departments organized and, above all, each teacher was to acquaint himself with the others.

As is inevitable in such faculty sessions, teachers being what they are, speeches brave and true were made. Henninger, for example pointed out to one and all that they were "brothers called to the great work of establishing an institution of learning for the training and education of teachers."

If one closely examines the minutes of these early faculty sessions, he will note with some satisfaction that the reply of the working teacher to this noble and clarion call involved the necessary and utilitarian minutia found in the everyday tasks of handling a class. They would want a dictionary for each room, cabinets for books, and above all, movable platforms for the front of each classroom so that they might not have to constantly stand.

Nevertheless, it was in these early meetings that the school was organized. It was not done without debate for there was great argument over whether the school organized for practice teaching would be called the "model" or the "practice" school. The first was discarded simply because it was "too strong a word," and the second was voted down because the word implied experimentalism. Eventually, and after much argument, this department of the Normal was named the Training School.[12]

Readers need not be reminded that the individuals taking part in these discussions were, for the most part, able and sincere people. Nevertheless it is true, as has been pointed out before, their appointments to the new faculty were made to a great extent upon political bases. As one contemporary put it: "current gossip was to the effect that appointments were on a party reward basis. . . each local school man who had a pull with a local member of the legislature got a job."[13]

The two limits of politics and experience by which appointments were made were not necessarily antipathetic, however, for it was possible to employ a good and seasoned teacher who, by coincidence, had the political pull required to get the job. One added point might be made, however; and that is, that the individuals chosen for the first faculty were experienced only on the high or grade school level. It was on that foundation that, although some of the new staff could pass as instructors for a college, the bulk of the new faculty was not as highly respected as it might have been.

Henninger himself was a good example of this problem. Though he appears as an enigma wrapped in a great mystery by reason of the lack of information concerning his nature, there is enough evidence to warrant some qualified assumptions about him. One person present at the time of the organization of the faculty, and particularly astute in observation remembers Henninger as being a prototype of his faculty, all of them being "more experienced in administration and teacher training than in subject matter." He was, she recalls, "conservative, perhaps a bit narrow in outlook, but intensely human and kindly in his attitude towards his students and other members of his faculty." He was, to some, a "fine man," handsome in appearance, average in weight and height.[14] Others simply saw him as quiet and genial, but not capable of "strong leadership." Above all, however, investigation proves him to have been primarily a politician. This is how he obtained the position of the presidency, this is how he kept it for approximately four years, and this is how he lost it in the end.[15]

Henninger's correspondence is full of notes to this local politico or that one; and though this was probably part of the responsibility of his office, it was not the only one. Here one may find a note to Len Small, a Kankakee politician who was later to become one of Illinois' most "colorful" governors, expressing a wish that the state representative would come to Macomb for a grand Washington's day gala which Henninger was arranging.

Again there is a note to another "pol," "an old acquaintance of mine" as Henninger describes him, inviting the gentleman to a tour of the campus. More than one individual had made the same mistake that Henninger made—that of tending the far off fences rather than those close to home. But there was one politician who remained outside of any of the blandishments which Henninger might have offered, and he lived in Macomb. This was L. Y. Sherman, and unfortunately as the new normal school president was to discover, he was really the man Henninger should have impressed. Instead, one finds time and again, ominous little notes from Sherman to Henninger that, had the latter really been politically aware, might have given him portent of things to come.[16]

IV.

There were variations on the theme with respect to other new appointees to the staff; and it seems mandatory to present an analysis of each character and personality.

There was Samuel B. Hursh, for example, who came to Western as its first teacher of English literature and grammar. He is described by one of his former students as having been a "true educator and an inspiration to all." Yet, he was a little more than that. Not every person could ever hope to achieve the level of genuine love and affection in which Mr. Hursh came to be held. He was, in essence, a colorful personality: a character who, when the golf course was built around the main building in these early years, would rise at dawn and play several rounds before his sleepy students sauntered upon the campus.

Nor was he one to conform. When a later president pronounced a strict dictum of no smoking upon the campus, Hursh obeyed but only within the outer confines of the regulation. He would stride down the middle of Adams Street, defying the impatient auto horns, holding his cigar in hand—neither on the campus or off. More than one student recalls how this magnificent man could hide a lighted cigar so cleverly upon his person that the only evidence was the slight panetella aroma left in his wake as he walked down the hall.

Basically, Hursh was an allegorist; a man of infinite story and verse. How well he could recall General Lee's invasion of Pennsylvania with the resultant battle of Gettysburg; and how, as a boy, he had to drive the family cattle into the hills to prevent their seizure by the invaders. These, and other stories, he would tell through a grand and glorious career which lasted into the late 1920's, when his retirement was soon followed by death.[17]

Almost from the same mold was James Burns, instructor in history and Latin, and a model for plain and simple ethical living for over twenty years at Western. Burns was a sturdy sort, whose ancestors were of Scottish and Ulster blood and who, like Hursh, came out of the hills of Pennsylvania. He was but eleven when the Civil War broke out, and as the years rolled by he would write with feeling of his life during those years of strife. He could well remember his brother's return from the war, and how through tear-flooded eyes he could "look back through the half-century and see the blue uniform . . . as he crossed the threshold."

Burns would later attend Monmouth College in Illinois, and there after graduation he would make his home, holding the position of Superintendent of the Monmouth Public Schools. He was, by all accounts, a kindly and gentle soul, and probably as ardent a scholar as ever held a seat of instruction at Western Illinois Normal. A teacher, he felt, was a person who should know—not just the price of coal, or how much the school furnace would use—but he should be aware of life. The whole wonder of man's glory and man's infamy should be laid bare for these young boys and girls from Pike and McDonough. The student must come to know the "glimpses of man's Asiatic beginnings," the glory that was Greece and the grandeur that was Rome's, and by doing so, he would know from whence man had come, and where he was going. Like Hursh, Burns taught at Western until the later 1920's, at which time he retired. Shortly thereafter he passed away.[18]

John Drake, who taught the physical sciences at Normal from the very beginning until his resignation in 1913, also came originally from the East. He was a lean and tall Yankee from Connecticut, and had been graduated from Connecticut Wesleyan in the mid-1890's. This was the same school at which Woodrow Wilson taught for some time, and one wonders if Drake might have been touched in some way by the wand of history. At any rate, his life seems to have been played upon by influences of a grand nature for, at the very time when science began to open the road of progress for all of mankind, Drake understood, even before many of his fellows, the nature of the kind of life to come.

There are those who recollect him as a far-seeing man who

told his classes in a reflective sort of way about the implication of the splitting of the atom, and what it might mean to the world. He could well do this, for in his graduate work at the University of Chicago and at the University of Wisconsin he had come under the tutelage of great and knowing men, such as Millikan and Bell. It may be written here that in the time of strong political influences upon the appointment and tenure of faculty members at Western, Drake survived longer than most. In the end, however, he would go, though unwillingly, to a position at the new normal school in Emporia, Kansas. Long after his leaving, people remembered this kindly man with an improper cast of eye and a New England accent, and his large and gracious home on Normal Street.[19]

Miss Cora Hamilton, appointed in 1902 as the supervisor of the training school for prospective teachers, also came from Connecticut. As was customary for her time, her teaching career began before she had finished high school. In fact, though she had just barely reached middle age upon coming to Western, she already had twenty-five years of teaching experience.

She was a handsome and portly woman who ate well, lived quietly and shunned physical exercise. Though she took up residence a slight distance from the place in which she labored, she always followed the practice of calling a taxi for conveyance. It was probably her ease of mind, her gentle ability for telling a fine story, and her love of life and beauty which brought her to long life; for it was in 1960 at the age of ninety-nine that she passed away. Her imprint is still on teacher training at Western, however, for along with her two assistants, Miss Laura Hazle and Miss Edith Keith, she established the foundations for such work in the institution. It was for this reason, and by virtue of her long years of service in the school, that her fine portrait hung with dignity in Simpkins Hall for many years.[20]

Mr. Frederick Fairbank and Miss Winifred Swartz were of a type different from their fellows. Both were very young, both were artistically inclined, and each was complementary to the other. Miss Swartz was a light, vivacious, and a gay sort, with a genuine love for the music which she taught in the new institution. She came to Macomb from Moline, where she had taught for a few years after her graduation from Winona State Normal in Minnesota.

Fairbank, on the other hand, was shy, introverted, scholarly (in fact he would later be released on the charge that he was too good for Western), loving the language arts which he taught at the Normal. He was a solid young man who, after his graduation from Illinois College in Jacksonville, Illinois, had obtained an M.A. from Yale.

It is comforting to know that each found solace in the other and that marriage was the result. Truly, the romance and its culmination is one of the highlights of the early years of Western, for to each student this was a perfect relationship of one man to one woman. It may be interesting to know that, until several years ago, Fairbank remained in good health and spirits, and that he lived at Portland, Oregon.[21]

Nor can the students of these early years forget the tall and dignified William J. Sutherland, instructor of geographic sciences at the new normal. Sutherland was born at Cherry Valley, Illinois, in 1865, and was graduated from Illinois State Normal in 1892. Later he acquired a bachelor's degree from the University of Wisconsin, after which he taught in various places in Illinois. All of those who remember him during his six years at Western recall his soft spoken voice and his easy grace, his expert ability in the difficult art of instruction, and his courtly way of dealing with people and problems. He was to all who knew him a gentleman all of the days of his life, which ended in suddenness in 1914 while he occupied the presidency of another normal school far distant in time and space from these early days in Macomb.[22]

Three other members of that first faculty appear to have been appointments strictly of a political nature. Mr. E. A. Wilkinson came to the school as an instructor of mathematics. He was a bachelor who had been graduated from Knox College just a few years before. After a stint of teaching at Knoxville, Illinois, he was employed at Western, a position which he held until his resignation in 1906.

Mr. H. L. Roberts, who taught biological science until 1906, appears along with Wilkinson as one whose appointment had a political coloration to it. He came originally from Ipava, a little village within hailing distance of Macomb, attending school at Otterbein College, Indiana University, and Illinois State Normal, pretty much in that order. He was a gentleman, easy in his ways and with his students. Though he remained just a few years in Macomb, almost all of those who remember him recall his habit of bringing his pet collie to class. The animal would coil up in front of his master's desk, only arousing himself to snap at the heels of students tardy in arrival to class.

Mr. S. L. Smith, the last of the first faculty to be mentioned here, was a genial and pleasant man who would also be relieved of his position in the great political sweep of 1906. During his short stay he was the art instructor at the institution.[23]

It may be of some interest to know the nature of salaries paid to these people in 1902. School boards, at this time, were never known to be neglectful of the financial interests of the taxpayer. A random selection of salaries paid at Western in the beginning shows that President Henninger was paid $291.66 per month (it would be difficult to reason the extra small change), Professor Hursch was given $200 a month, and Miss Dunbar, who came a little later as librarian, received $45 a month. When Henninger resigned in 1905, the Board, waiting for Alfred Bayliss to ready himself for the presidency of the institution, employed Mr. Hursch to act as temporary president. Members of the Board then strictly of a local nature, were quick to point out publicly that Hursch would be paid only $200 more per year for the added responsibility, thus "saving the school $3,400." Parenthetically, further money seems to have been saved in the employment of the janitorial staff. Ed DeCamp, the colorful and popular caretaker, received only $45 per month for his duties.[24]

V.

On the morning of September 23, 1902, the same Ed DeCamp, then a young man and Western's first janitor, strode purposefully to the front door of what is now called Sherman Hall. In his hand he carried a simple but treasured family heirloom—nothing more than a hand bell which had been used by his mother some years before when she had been a country school teacher. He shook it vigorously, calling into session and into being the first of many generations of students to be taught at the new normal. He was a proud man, DeCamp was, and for many years he kept that bell, knowing that somehow, and in a small way, he had been part of the history of his times. Much he would forget before his retirement thirty-eight years later, but this he would not. It was indelibly printed upon his mind—the ringing of the bell, the new students, the freshness of the day, and the sense of his youth and being.[25]

There were others who were quite proud to be a part of the occasion. The new faculty, aware that the building would not tumble tomorrow or the day after that, sensed an importance to this moment in history. The building would survive all of them, and many more after them; but it was important that they were the first. By being so, they would always be remembered. Not that they appreciated the words and description of the *Macomb Journal* which portrayed them as a "well oiled machine," with each member of the faculty dropping "into the places assigned to them." But they, too, noted with the *Journal* that President Henninger appeared as a purposeful figure, striding up and down the halls, directing personnel this way and that, and playing his new role to the ultimate. And Henninger, himself, would read the *Journal* with pride, agreeing with its description of the new school's "elaborate, yet . . . not cheap or shoddy" furniture.[26]

The most important fact of all was that the students were now beginning to appear. Much to the surprise of almost everyone, a more than anticipated number of young men and women registered. Without luggage in some instances, or without lodging in others, they came from Baldinsville, Ipava, and other nearby towns. Professor Burns, a willing and thoughtful soul, spent more than a few hours waiting patiently for trains to arrive so that he might help the prospective scholars to find rooms or facilities.

This was a difficult task, for Macomb had its customary housing shortage even in those days. Eventually President Henninger made a personal appeal to householders to rent rooms to incoming students. When he had exhausted the supply of public spirited citizens, he called for help from those with other facets of character. By charging fifty cents a room per week, and by renting one room to two students, one could make as much as a dollar a week![27]

For those students who found rooms and who stayed, the last week in September was a thrilling and exciting one. With great dignity and pomp, as well as with occasional circumstance, they were all called together in the unfinished gymnasium which, in that innocent age, was decorated with goldenrod. The students were subjected to many preachments—the "dos and don'ts" of college living—and fortified with moral strictures concerning behavior on the streets of the town.[28]

Autumns are beautiful in Western Illinois; they are the one concession which Mother Nature allows that part of the state. This particular September may have been overly endowed with color; at least that was how one student of the time remembered it. The tall and graceful elms had turned into beige, and the sugar maples, which are plentiful in Western Illinois, cast a golden glow wherever they stood. The Norwegian Maples added a Tintoretto red to the woods along the Lamoine River. The same senior citizen, then in her glory years, now remembers the first week of school at the Normal with both nostalgia and some slight embarrassment. She was introduced to her gymnasium uniform—"voluminous dark blue bloomers, middy blouse with sailor collar, and long black stockings." But then, as she was inclined to describe it, the spirit of the new school was one of youth. A maidenly blush was a necessary and accepted aspect of the time and the place.[29]

So the classes began. There was a variety of them, as was to be expected, for like most institutions of its type, the Western Normal curriculum ran the gamut from high school to college courses. All were part of the same system, for in those days it was possible for a student to enroll for four years of high school and college classes; the end result of which was a certificate which qualified him to teach in the better high schools of the state.

IV.

The school was divided into the departments of psychology and school management, English, history and civics, geography and geology, mathematics, physics and chemistry, library and reading, Latin and German, music and physical culture, drawing and penmanship, the training school, and methods work. A student ordinarily took six courses a term, with electives appearing on his schedule in the second year of his college level course. There was, in fact, a surprising number of possible electives listed in the earliest catalogs—some forty in all. But one may suspect that, as in many catalogs of that period and now, the subjects were listed but rarely taught.

High school graduates intending to enter the school were expected to have the recommendation of their county superintendents, as well as statements of good conduct from various citizens in their respective communities. It was emphasized again and again in the literature distributed by the Normal that students were to be of "high moral character."

One may well wonder about the scholarship abilities of these early students, or about the calibre of many of their instructors. One clever and astute faculty gentleman who came in 1907, and whose word should carry some weight, remembers that the school lacked considerably in polish mainly because it started on too "meager a basis." The building did not offer the proper facilities, he writes; it lacked a good library, and the quarters were "inadequate."

When Professor Burns met his first class, one entitled "Methods in American History," he found that the students were so unconscionably unprepared that they did not know the "elementary facts" of America's past. A student of this period, still an active alert alumna of the institution, remembers that there were a few good college level courses taught by the early faculty, among them those handled by Roberts and Fairbank. Readers might be reminded at this point, however, that the latter was later dismissed on the basis that he was simply "too good" to teach at Western. The same alumna, remarking further about the lack of true college level approach in these early days, concludes that "this was probably not surprising in view of the standards of normal schools sixty years ago." [30]

Withal, however, it is difficult to assess the standards of any period in the history of a school, even after the passage of several decades. As with many colleges, there have been hard and perilous moments in Western's past. Times came when accusations were freely made in heat and anger concerning standards in the school; some claiming that they were too low, others asserting that they were too high. Good judgment will determine, however, that standards are usually set not so much by faculty and administration, but by time and circumstance. When they rise or fall in Macomb, the same relative movement takes place at Michigan State University or at the City College of New York. No faculty member, no matter how great his emotions or effort, can swim with ease against the tide of public morality or public indifference.

At Western Illinois Normal in 1902, standards were scarcely different from those of Illinois State Normal, the oldest of the normal schools in the state. It is indeed possible that the quality of the student body in Macomb was superior to that in Carbondale, where the second oldest normal school in the state was located. At any rate, during the first eight years of Western's history, instructors having credits from both older normals were employed to teach in Macomb.

While one writer, in describing the same period of time at Southern Illinois Normal, has pridefully expressed that the Carbondale institution was far ahead of the "common run of normal school," there is yet considerable evidence to the contrary.[31] Textbooks written by Charles DeGarmo, C. C. Van Liew, and Charles McMurry were used both in Macomb and Carbondale. Western Illinois already had a long tradition of the excellent private college in Knox, Illinois College, and Monmouth College. In Sutherland, the geography instructor, and in Dickerson, who would come later, Western had some published professors during its first decade.

It might be admitted that Western's first students lacked the polish of students at Knox, at Urbana, or at Normal. The reason for this was simple, and it lay in the fact that all three of the latter schools were older and were based in larger towns. Henninger himself admitted the ingenuousness and naivete of Western's first class, and blamed it upon the pressure to fill the school at any cost. As the new President wrote to his friend, De-Garmo, only fifty percent of the Western students came from well equipped high schools, and few of the young people, if any, had superior backgrounds.[32]

There was no lack of effort on the part of students or faculty, however. The former read their textbooks which included Channing's *History of the United States,* Fiske's *Civil Government,* and Well's *Essentials of Plane and Solid Geometry.*[33] By the time that Miss Ora Zuck and Miss Maude McAdams were graduated in 1903 to the strains of "appropriate music," the school was well on its way to a firm intellectual base.

Miss Zuck, the first of the two to be graduated, went the way of her training into a long teaching career. It was her privilege to see Western grow from an idea into reality.[34] By 1903, for example, the school was committed to a summer term. Miss Zuck probably also read the *Clionian,* a brisk and effective college newspaper.[35] She very likely also sang the school song of the time, "Mid the Gently Rolling Prairies;" a piece written by her classmate, Miss Mary Murphy, at the suggestion of Mrs. Henninger. The song, only heard rarely now, is to be differentiated from "We're Marching On," a fight song written later by Walter Piety Morgan and W. H. Eller.[36]

Miss Zuck, Miss Murphy, or Miss McAdams may well have strolled to the old well which was located on what is now the southwest corner of Tillman Hall. The well remained a part of the tradition of the school for several decades.

If there is a point to this reminiscence, it is that, by 1904, there was already a love affair between the institution and its students. The attraction of the latter to the place existed in spite of the inadequacies of the faculty or the building itself. Many of the school's early graduates felt a shimmer of emotion decades later when hearing the song which praised the "gold without a stain, the purple queenly still." As one young man phrased it: "Western, you are beautiful because you are surrounded by nature. . . . Your elm trees spread out their stately branches and seem quietly to say to all humanity—come hither and rest in my cool shade and I will protect you."[37]

Chapter II: *The Henninger Era*

1. Caroline Grote, "The Normal Schools of Illinois," *School News*, July, 1911, pp. 512-513.

2. *Courier*, Mar. 20, 1925.

3. *Ibid.*

4. *Ibid.* Many early pictures show the planks stretching from Adams Street to the front doors of Sherman Hall.

5. *Macomb Journal*, Sept. 25, 1902.

6. *Ibid.* Early pictures show burnished woods, and combination gas and electric light fixtures.

7. *Courier*, Mar. 20, 1925. Students of the 1903 period complained about the noise made by the workmen in finishing the auditorium. Many people still remember watching buckets of cement being hauled up past their classroom windows while classes were in session.

8. James Grigsby, a present Vice-President of W.I.U., is the source of part of this information.

9. Schlesinger, *op. cit.*, p. 168.

10. Harper, *op. cit.*, p. 125.

11. *Ibid.*, pp. 103-104. Oliver Dickerson wrote to me some time ago that the system of teacher certification in use at this time was quite efficient, and that he had to wait for the "improved reading" techniques of later years to find students who couldn't read.

12. Information from handwritten minutes of early faculty meetings now in possession of Central Administration, W.I.U. Professor Burns was the first faculty secretary.

13. Communication from Oliver Dickerson, Feb., 1961.

14. Letter from Mrs. J. B. Glasgow, Dec., 1961.

15. Others described him as "austere," quiet, and orderly. *Macomb Journal*, Sept. 25, 1902, described him as "progressive, cultured . . . a fluent and ready speaker. . . ." He was a strong Methodist, and opposed dancing, smoking, and drinking.

16. Len Small to Henninger, Feb. 20, 1903; L. Y. Sherman to Henninger, March 10, 1903. Sherman warned Henninger against no "funny work," and that the President should get accounts straightened out. Letters to be found in *Presidents' Collection*, to be found in basement of Sherman Hall.

17. Letter from Mr. Guy Hoyt, Feb. 15, 1961.

18. Prof. Burns' papers, now in Central Administration Offices, W.I.U.

19. *Journal*, Sept. 25, 1902. Prof. Drake's son, who was an official with the E.C.A. in Washington during the 1960's, was instrumental in sending a number of Nigerian students to the school in 1962 and 1963.

20. Letter from Mr. Guy Hoyt, Feb. 15, 1961. Mr. Hoyt described Miss Hamilton as a "story teller without peer."

21. *Journal*, Sept. 25, 1902.

22. *Ibid.*

23. *Ibid.*

24. Henninger to J. H. Pollock, Oct. 30, 1902, *Presidents' Collection.*

25. *Courier,* Dec. 16, 1933; *Sequel,* 1940.

26. *Ibid.*

27. Written to me by Mrs. J. B. Glasgow, the daughter of James Burns.

28. *Ibid.*

29. Mrs. Martha McLean Davis to Miss Susan Davies, April 27, 1961; now in my possession.

30. Letter from O. M. Dickerson, Feb., 1961. Also communications from Mrs. Glasgow.

31. George K. Plochmann, *The Ordeal of Southern Illinois University,* p. 380.

32. Henninger to DeGarmo, Dec. 15, 1902, *Presidents' Collection.*

33. *Summer Catalog,* W.I.N.S., 1903.

34. Henninger to Terry, May 5, 1902, *Presidents' Collection.*

35. *Clionian,* Feb., 1905. Miss Zuck's first teaching position was in Chicago Heights, Illinois.

36. Henninger to Searle, Mar. 6, 1903, *Presidents' Collection.* Henninger wrote: "Our faculty are willing to undergo many inconveniences and discomforts if they can help the School increase its grip on the patronizing territory."

37. *Courier,* May 19, 1922. There was a large variety of trees on the campus by 1922—a Maidenhair tree near Adams Street, a Bald Cypress near Lake Ruth (still there), Larch and Tamarack near Sherman Hall, and Butternut in front of campus. A Biology Department survey of several years ago listed several pages of different trees, single spaced. Charles Finley, a Western faculty member who later became a prominent biologist at Columbia University, counted eighty-six species of birds in the early part of 1917 on Western's campus.

Bayliss Wins Out

As any good politician knows, those who live by the sword in the world of politics may well die from it. President Henninger was undoubtedly a politician of sorts. Being so, he must have been aware that the position he had obtained through manipulation might be taken from him by the same means.

Truly, by the middle of 1905 Henninger's time was drawing to a close. He had finished several difficult years of leadership. The main building was not yet finished, and the auditorium was not in a state of readiness. The locally appointed Board of Trustees had openly expressed disappointment in Henninger and seemed to feel that the faculty could be of better quality.

But behind it all was the political situation, and Macomb's most powerful politician, L. Y. Sherman. Frank Harris, who for many years edited Macomb's largest newspaper, described the situation years later thusly: Henninger was Governor Yates' choice for the Western position, but when Yates was succeeded by the pro-Sherman Governor Deneen, Henninger's days were numbered.

It was not that Henninger was a bad president, Harris concluded. The man had done the best he could with what he had. He had shown good qualities of organization, but the fact of the matter was that he would always be opposed by the Sherman element. Henninger didn't really have a chance. This was Sherman's home town and territory and, when the local politician got his chance, Henninger had to go.[1]

The chance came when Deneen moved into the Governor's Mansion and Sherman, as a reward for this support, was given control of political spoils in the Macomb area. Within days after the Governor's inauguration Sherman named a new Board of Trustees, and the Board in turn proceeded to ask for Henninger's resignation.

The result was a shock wave which spread across the campus. Students first became aware of these proceedings when the *Courier*, the old *Clionian* renamed, broke the story. "A new Board of Trustees has been appointed," proclaimed the newspaper, "the old President has resigned, a new President has been elected, a temporary President chosen, a new architect appointed. . . ."

Furthermore, the *Courier* continued, a new atmosphere had been created under acting-President Hursh. Workmen were putting effort into finishing the building, guttering was being hung, and sodding and seeding of the lawn was underway. And, wonder of wonders, the electricians appeared to be anxious to finish the wiring of the building.[2]

Hursh was acting in the role of caretaker. Alfred E. Bayliss was the new President, in fact, but he had delayed his arrival in Macomb in order to clear his obligations elsewhere. Hursh did his new duties well, however, for it was during this brief span of time that he commenced the task of beautifying the campus. With the help and support of a member of the Board, Mr. John Keefer, he undertook the work with great diligence. Care was taken in the selection of species of trees to be planted on the campus, with a nod of favoritism going to the birches. These white-barked trees were planted along the walks in front of the new building and, in time, they became a source of pride for a whole generation of Western students.[3]

It may also be added that Keefer, himself, was responsible for the creation of one of Western's landmarks. To the southwest of Sherman, where a ravine runs off in the direction of Adams Street, Keefer placed a dam and planted trees. The little pond which resulted was named after Keefer's daughter, Ruth.

Bayliss took over the actual administration of the school early in 1906, and it was not long before this remarkable man went into action. The axe came down in June, and almost all of the original faculty were dismissed. Again it was the *Courier* which produced the most colorful report of the affair. While high sounding phrases common to graduation ceremonies were bouncing off nearby walls, "six noble geniuses," the Board of Trustees, sat in a room on the third floor. One of the gentlemen present was a "character half seated in his chair, half reclining on the table, pouring forth his brilliant ideas."[4]

"Who is this man?" the editor asked. "He is the Honorable President of W.I.S.N.S.." The implication of the student writer was there for all to see. Bayliss had wanted a new faculty from the Board of Trustees, and he was getting it.

Before that June day came to an end, a new era had begun for Western. Bayliss's bold maneuvers were fraught with dangers for many of the dismissed instructors had built popular followings in Macomb and among the student body. The removal of Burns brought numerous repercussions, for he had been somewhat "of a father" to many students from outlying areas. Fortunately for Burns and the school, however, he eventually returned to the institution after a lapse of several years. Parenthetically, one of the charges made against this popular man by the Board in 1906 was that he had failed to properly teach a Sunday school class, and that his religious ideas were too "progressive."

The reaction on the behalf of young Fairbank was also strong. Unlike some of his colleagues, this instructor had acquired a highly respected graduate degree. One might suspect, in looking at the record, that the dismissal of Fairbank by Bayliss may have been part of a rare display of impetuosity by the

new President. It is possible that Bayliss wished to sweep the
faculty clean of undesirable elements and Fairbank just happened to get in the way. On the other hand, however, Fairbank
may have been the price that Bayliss had to pay in order to move
the others out, for the person chosen to fill the vacancy in foreign languages was none other than a niece of one of the Board
members.[5]

All in all, this part of the proceedings was most difficult
for Bayliss to justify. Newspapers in Western Illinois made
much of the statement of one of the Board members that Fairbank was just "too good" for the school and that the Board
could save money by employing a "mediocre" teacher. For the
other dismissals Bayliss had an answer. He was a man of few
words; indeed, in many cases, just one. His reason for the multiple firings was simple and direct. It was "expediency." And for
the sake of the same reason Fairbank also had to go.

Expediency is a word which may carry broad implications.
In the years which followed, it is clearly seen that, Fairbank
aside, the new President intended to build a school of quality.
Many of the older faculty did not fit his vision of educational
respectability. Also, it was with the understanding that he
should have the right to remove undesirable faculty members
that he took the president's office. In the immediate sense there
were some hard feelings and unnecessary hardships, but in the
long run the institution would be the beneficiary of a marked
improvement in standards.

It was true that the opposition would continue to snipe at
Bayliss from time to time, but such could not be unexpected.
The *Courier*, for example, bitterly concluded: "Woe to that
member of the faculty who is a friend of ex-Governor Yates, ex-
President Henninger, or who in any other way has shown an-
tagonism to Judge Sherman or Superintendent Bayliss!" That
Fairbank, Burns, and others had to go, the paper added, was an
act completely representative of "petty politics, the curse of

democracy."[6]

What the editor of the *Courier* failed to note, however, was the fact that he was allowed to freely express his disagreement with the policies of the school. There, in itself, was a sign of the character of the Bayliss years. The broad and generous man who now occupied the president's chair understood far more about real democracy than many of the young people who now criticized him. They would continue to have great freedom for expression and growth in the next eight years. Acting with those rights they would become citizens worthy of testing the great "American dream."

II.

As has been implied, Alfred E. Bayliss was a most amazing man. Born in Gloucestershire, England, in 1847, he was brought by his parents to Michigan at the age of six. Put on his own at the age of twelve, he managed to work his way through the Hillsdale Academy in Michigan; an experience which apparently tempered and changed his life. In 1863, at the age of sixteen, he enlisted in the 11th Michigan Cavalry, and managed to get into some fairly stiff military action. He was present at the capture of Jefferson Davis, at the close of the war; an experience which he always recalled with zeal.[7]

Sixteen was such a young age for the hard activities of the Civil War, and Bayliss was profoundly affected by these years of growth. He always wore his Grand Army of the Republic button, and occasionally told his student audiences about the problems of growing up while in uniform. On one occasion he was hanged by his thumbs for twelve hours for some minor indiscretion.

But this was the most emotional of all of America's conflicts and, inevitably, the young men who participated in it would regard their roles in the conflict as not lacking in relevance or significance in the creation of a new America. As men like Bay-

liss grew heavier with weight, years, and wisdom, they re-
counted their experiences like the beads of some rosary and with
considerable emotion.

Upon his return to civilian life, Bayliss entered the teaching
profession and eventually became the principal of LaGrange
High School in Indiana. Four years later he moved to Mt. Sterling, Illinois, where he filled the role of Superintendent of
Public Schools. Shortly thereafter he left teaching and became a
newspaper editor, which gradually involved him in the state
political scene. In time he was elected as the State Superintendent of Public Instruction, a position which he used as a
springboard to the presidency at Western.

In every sense of the word, as his career at Western shows,
he was an admirable man. Sixty years later there are still significant bits of evidence about to prove that this was so. Primarily,
however, one must rely principally upon Bayliss's own words,
and the estimates made of him by people who lived long after
the man's death. On one occasion he stated quite simply the
nature of his goal as Western's chief executive. "If I could be
sure of ten years of administration, I should not fear much for
for the results," he explained.

As fate would have it, he did not have ten years. He only
had eight, and the tragedy of his time was that he did not live
out a decade of administration. Those two unfulfilled years
were to influence the character of the school for decades to come.

Bayliss was not a fluent man, though this acted as no great
handicap. On occasion, however, he would combine an innate
prudence which was the principal mark of his character with
some appealing emotion to produce oratory worth noting. Once
to a group of schoolteachers he said:

> The truth is, we can never sell life for a price. Make the real
> price nothing if you would receive all. Pray only for elbow room,
> insight, courage, strength, and leave to work. It is the peculiarity
> of our work that in a very large sense is its own continuing re-

ward. . . . You will not hurry, neither will you rest. As well try to
hurry the stars in their courses as to hurry life.[8]

Much was written and much was said upon the occasion of
his death a few years later for, indeed, all of Macomb and the
Military Tract went into mourning at his unexpected demise.
The great John Williston Cook, President of Northern Illinois
Normal and himself an influence in American education, recalled that particular moment when he heard of Bayliss's appointment at Western. "The problems of Macomb Normal are
well on the way toward solution when Alfred Bayliss takes hold
of them," he told a friend. "You watch Macomb and see it come
out all right."[9] And the Western faculty memorialized at Bayliss's death:

> In his relations with his associates he exhibited rare patience and
> was most kind. He never allowed anyone to exceed him in
> generosity, and always praised the virtues of the unappreciated.
> . . . With the subtlest tactfulness he wove the threads of per-
> sonal divergence into a fabric of happy companionship with the
> delicacy of genius. So perfect were his adjustments with the mem-
> bers of his faculty that none felt the slightest restraint.[10]

There are other revealing pictures of the man. One elderly
citizen remembered Bayliss as a more demanding man than his
predecessor, but still kindly and forbearing in his behavior. He
really never wished to be called "president" but preferred the
more egalitarian term of "principal." This was an element of
his character which shaded his innate sense of modesty. Nor did
he ever refer to the school which he administered as anything
else but "The Military Tract Normal School," a title far more
inclusive than its real one.

On the occasion of his death, Professor Hursh undertook an
analysis of his character; a task for which Hursh was eminently
qualified. Bayliss was a man of quiet and subtle intellect, Hursh
asserted, though he was not brilliant in the sense of having a
quicksilver mind. He never replied quickly or made snap judg-

ments. Nor did Bayliss speak for effect, but rather he took a course "measured" by thought and reflection.

There were some, Hursh continued, who thought Bayliss to be cold and distant. Yet, this was only his outward defense against accusations of faculty favoritism. He truly had a sub-terranean character, full of shadows and meanings like that of a deep underground cave. There were, Hursh concluded, a few yardsticks to Bayliss's character. He was an administrator with an inborn "mingling of caution and modesty, often mistaken for timidity." His worst misfortune was to be "misunderstood by those who caught only a fragment of his meaning or pur-pose." Furthermore, Hursch eulogized, "if he ever fired off a sky rocket it was done with a long and slow fuse which allowed him to get so far away that some mere passer-by usually got the credit and glory of the demonstration."[11]

Oliver M. Dickerson, one of the ablest and most scholarly of the Western faculty in the Bayliss era, recalled his President as a rather interesting combination of tact and executive ability. Bayliss, he wrote, was determined from the beginning to over-come the handicaps under which the school labored. The new President's major aim was to choose a competent staff. "He had a quiet and orderly habit," Dickerson added. And, as for campus life, the eminent historian remembered:

> Under President Bayliss, the Normal school was a very close knit organization. There was no friction between faculty members, each having his own particular work. That promoted growth. President Bayliss and his family were sociable, and made them-selves the center of the life of the group; and there were dinners and much informal activity. Students knew the faculty person-ally. Social life with the leading people of Macomb was cordial. No one accused the faculty of being kept apart from the rest of the town.[12]

III.

If comparisons were to be made about Western's past, it would seem difficult to find a better situation than that which

existed during the Bayliss period. Some instructors were retained from those employed during the Henninger administration but, in most cases, Bayliss simply went out and found the
type of person which best fitted his estimate of what Western
Illinois most needed.

The new faculty additions were people with solid academic
backgrounds. Understanding this aspect of the Bayliss policy, it
becomes quite clear that if he had lived longer than he did, the
school would be quite different than it is today. Oliver Dickerson related how he was employed:

> Personally I did not even know that there was an opening in
> Macomb. I was busy clearing up the final details of my work for
> the Ph.D. degree. One day he (Bayliss) walked into my work room
> in the library, introduced himself and offered me a position as
> head of the History Department. There was no application, no
> references. I understood that other members of the staff were
> selected the same way.[13]

Thus it was that Bayliss employed a new faculty. He presented the names of new appointments to the Board, obtained
its approval, and then published the list. "In this way he
avoided any effort to apply political pressures on him in the
selection of his staff," remembered a staff member of the time.[14]

Dickerson was the prize addition to the faculty in the
Bayliss era. Students who attended Western between 1906 and
1914 remember him as a tall and quite handsome man who had
the slightest of a Scots accent. Dickerson, while he resided in
Macomb, published the first of many books to come from his
pen (a new edition of the same book was printed in 1963). And
he eventually became the foremost expert on colonial history in
the United States.

His career in the field of colonial research, his excellent
record in World War I, his presidency of the American Historical Association, plus other achievements brought him international recognition. At the time of his death just a few years

ago he was listed in almost every "Who's Who" of significance, including that which listed internationally known individuals.

His resignation from Western in 1914, before he had won any of these honors, was a most unfortunate occurrence for the school, for more than anything else it signified a repudiation of deep scholarship by the Board. The tragedy of Dickerson's departure is that it was probably done with some unwillingness on his part, and with the feeling that he could not stay in view of the changing philosophy of the institution with regard to normal school training.[15]

Another significant addition to the staff after 1906 was that of Frederick Bonser. Like Dickerson he was a handsome and casual man whose dealings with students and colleagues were easy and gracious. He was the kind of person who took a great interest in many aspects of school life—always poking about here and there, and spending a great deal of his time with his Filipino students, about whom more will be written later.

In some rather mystical fashion Bonser managed to instill in his students a kind of messianic zeal about teaching. He dragged visiting instructors down to shop classes held in the basement of the school. Students admired him and were quite naturally shaken when their hero, importuned by the newly created Columbia Teachers College, left Macomb after a few years in order to advance his career. In New York City he became rather famous, along with his colleagues Dewey and Kilpatrick, and, when he died in the late 1920's, Columbia printed a special dedicatory edition of Bonser's writings.

It may be added here, parenthetically, that if Bonser had stayed in Macomb, he might have become the next president of Western Illinois Normal. As fate decreed, when Bayliss died, his successor was John McGilvrey, who was Bonser's replacement.[16]

When Bonser went to Columbia, he took with him two of Western's more able pedagogy instructors. These were Miss

Mable Carney and Miss Lois Coffee, both of whom were added to the staff in the Bayliss period. The latter was a strong willed woman who, during her stay in Macomb, transformed the *Courier* into an interesting and literate weekly publication. When she left, her place was taken by Miss Mabel Corbin. Though Miss Coffee was an extremely vital person, little was really lost in her departure for her replacement was every bit her match in integrity and energy.

Miss Carney was an acute and perceptive individual, and the type for whom Bayliss so ardently searched when staffing his faculty. There is ample evidence of her character in the single fact that almost sooner than anyone else in her time, she foresaw the demise of the country school. Yet, while in Macomb, she taught the "country school" curriculum at Western, and established a so-called model country school a few miles out of town.*

If one reads the *Couriers* published in 1906, he comes up with the essence of her philosophy in regard to rural education. First it was the duty of the normal schools to provide the kind of trained teachers necessary for country schools, she argued; and secondly, it was the duty of society to abolish such schools as soon as possible. "Consolidation," she concluded, "is the one and only solution."[17]

It is very understandable that the loss of both Miss Coffee and Miss Carney was regrettable, and a blow to Western's reputation as a normal school. Both women became nationally known in their respective fields while at Columbia, yet both women continued some association with Macomb for the remainder of their lives. Miss Coffee passed away some time ago, but Miss Carney lived until 1969 when she died at Evanston, Illinois.

Three other additions by Bayliss after 1906 were Susie B. Davis, Nina Lamkin, and Maud Shamel. Miss Davis was, as de-

---

* Miss Carney, years later, came back to Illinois in order to join the staff of I.S.N.U.

scribed by those who knew her, a "real find." It is very likely that Western has seldom seen her equal in terms of initiative and drive. She was, in a real sense, a source of pride for Macomb, for her productions of Shakespearian drama were of singularly high quality. It was Miss Davis who, when she tired of the acoustical horrors of the auditorium, took her plays to the outdoors. And it was Miss Davis who established the open air theater in the ravine to the east of the school; a landmark which remained in use probably to the end of the 1930's.

Miss Davis left in 1914 along with the others, apparently discontented with the changes which took place with the appointment of Walter Piety Morgan to the presidency. She became, for a while, a teacher of drama in the Milwaukee public school system, but then eventually found her way back into university instruction. It was 1935 before she again performed on the stage at Western with a series of readings on great Americans. At that time she was a highly respected member of the faculty of the University of Wisconsin, and the Dean of Women at the same institution.[18]

Miss Lamkin, who taught physical education for women while at Western, was a brilliant exponent of her field as well as a most excellent instructor. Almost every student of this period who still lives remembers her exceptional ability to organize school programs involving physical training. When, as the others had done, she left the school in 1914, she became one of the more admired leaders of her profession, becoming nationally known both as a lecturer and an author. Eventually, she became the Director of the Department of Physical Education at Northwestern University, a position which she held for quite some time. After her retirement she lived in Florida where she passed away in the late 1950's.[19]

Miss Shamel was Bayliss's appointment in the field of music instruction. Her abilities can best be described by an alumnus who remembers her in this manner:

There was a treat for the unsophisticated eyes of the country boys. She had light reddish hair and a splendid figure by anyone's judgment. And could she get music-singing out of us boys and girls! You must remember that those country boys and girls had heard no real music until we got to Macomb. I am sure that most of us old-timers would agree that she and many of the other faculty people gave us a good start on our way toward appreciation of the truly enriching experience of life.[20]

Margaret Dunbar, a fine librarian who had been appointed to the staff by President Henninger, was allowed to stay on. As good as she was, however, she could not keep pace with the great amount of work required of the position. The library in 1906 appeared in a sorry state, for books lay in that east and second floor room unstacked and uncatalogued. Recognizing the difficulties involved, Bayliss appointed Miss Fanny Jackson as an assistant to Miss Dunbar, and the two women worked overtime to remedy the situation. By 1909 this department was as big and as efficient as one could expect in a library of an institution of Western's size.

Miss Dunbar left in the 1914 exodus; in her case, in order to fill an appointment on the staff of the newly established Kent State College in Ohio. Today, one of the buildings of that fine school is named after this woman, a further testimony to the types of losses suffered when Western's faculty broke apart in the early years of the Morgan administration. Miss Jackson stayed on, though, and served out her many years at Western with distinction and loyalty.[21]

There were still other exceptional appointments by Bayliss after 1906. John T. Johnson, for example, established the first real agricultural program with his experimental soil plots. Soil fertility and seed selection were this man's specialities, and he was so good at them that he eventually became the subject of another internecine raid pulled off by Kent State in 1914.

Another Bayliss addition was Miss Blenda Olson. Miss Olson was of Swedish stock, coming to this country at the age of eleven. Later she was graduated from the University of Illinois, majoring in foreign languages, and continued her long studies in the field with work at the University of Grenoble and at the Sorbonne. Along with Miss Olson, and the previously mentioned Miss Corbin, came Eva Colby, another product of the Bayliss revolution. Until her retirement in the 1930's, Miss Colby acted as the kind and thoughtful head of a burgeoning home economics department. Such was this woman's appeal that this area of studies became so overwhelmed with students that other departments were dwarfed by its size.[22]

It is left now to discuss the last of Bayliss's additions to Western's 1906 faculty—Miss Caroline Grote. This great woman, after whom the oldest of the women's dormitories is named, came to the school after a long and able career in public school teaching in Pike County. Many are the adjectives called to mind by those who knew her. She was to all students a "marvelous example." She was "understanding," and approachable by reason of that rare empathy which students instinctively recognized.

Her colleagues knew her as a "solid, motherly type," a woman with long teaching experience, and as that rare specimen, a politically-minded and practical woman who knew Western Illinois as intimately as any male politician of her time. As an undergraduate she attended Carthage College in Illinois, and as a graduate student the University of Chicago and Columbia Teachers College. Long past the age when others might have given up the goal, she continued work toward the Ph.D. at Columbia. She finally achieved it. No task was too small for her attention, and no student unworthy of her time. Needless to say, her lifetime in college teaching was spent in Macomb, for even if she had been able, she would never have left this part of the country. Her roots were here, and to this place she dedicated her life.[23]

Not all of Henninger's faculty was removed, as stated before. Those whom Bayliss admired were kept. These included

Hursh, who continued on as a Richelieu to this President as well as to the one who succeeded him; Sutherland, that tall and scholarly gentleman who stayed on in geography until called to the presidency of Platteville Normal in Wisconsin; and Drake in physics and chemistry.

IV.

The Bayliss years were not spectacular ones in terms of school expansion. A study of the period shows a steady but firm growth both in curricula and size of student body, and a rock deep consolidation of what had already come to be accepted as part of the Western tradition. There were, by 1908, some one hundred and forty-six graduates of the school, most of them following a teaching career. By the end of the Bayliss era, 1911, registration figures showed some two hundred and sixty women and one hundred and forty-one men in the normal school course, and one hundred and seventy-five boys and girls in the training school.[24]

The two year course in "principles of education" still existed in the normal school curriculum, but slight changes had occurred elsewhere. There was the "country school" course which required one year of study, as well as a variety of extension courses; a specialty in which the school pioneered. In that year classes were taught in Moline, Rock Island, Quincy, Mt. Sterling, Peoria, and Pittsfield.[25] So great did the burden of the program become that Bayliss employed John McGilvrey for the purpose of administering the program.

McGilvrey, who briefly succeeded to the presidency later, was a slender and gentle man; a good administrator who eventually left Western to take the position of the presidency of Kent State College in Ohio.

The Bayliss years, once again, were good years. In a period before great world conflict and pressing international problems, Americans could still live with comfort as well as grace. A

vigorous and forceful Theodore Roosevelt presided over a
people imbued with a concept that the United States, freedom,
and democracy were synonymous. When Filipino students appeared upon Western's campuses in these years, they were welcomed as prospective teachers of the American ethic; as mis-
sionaries of the American dream.

This all began when Mrs. James Burns, the wife of the
school's first history instructor and a woman who had spent
some time in the Orient, invited a group of Filipinos to
Macomb. By 1906 there were six of them at the school.
They kept coming until well into the 1920's.

All of them were good students and all were grateful
for this exceptional opportunity for self improvement. While
at Western they won oratorical contests, they edited the
Courier, they played football, they attended banquets at the
homes of their professors, and they dreamed of applying
Bonserian principles to the students of their homeland.

Many of them became prominent men in their own society in years to come. Some became college presidents, and
others became school administrators. One, Basilio Vargas,
became the Assistant Regional Superintendent of the Bureau
of Private Schools in the Philippine Republic. Another, Dr.
Camilio Osias, became a member of the Senate of his country.[26]

Most of these young men took fond memories of Western Illinois home with them. There was skating in winter
on the newly filled Lake Ruth, and there were sleighrides
in the country. They were welcome guests at school banquets where all present, students and professors alike, threw
off most of their inhibitions. They studied the strange habits
of Americans and the difficulty of the language (the entire
1909 *Sequel* was printed with simplified spelling—a Bayliss
experiment). And there were those wonderful programs in
the auditorium.

This great room, finally finished in 1906, was dedicated

with appropriate ceremonies in April of the same year. On that night of nights Macomb was treated to a heady dose of culture which included Mendelssohn's *Elijah,* performed to the tune of folding chairs scraping on a wooden floor, and by a soprano who, according to the local newspaper, was not at her "best." The girl was suffering from an attack of "nervous indigestion."[27]

It all seemed grand, however, especially with the baroque plaster impressions about the stage and ceiling, and the large and impressive paintings on the walls. True, the local newspaper reviewed the whole business as a bit "heavy" in both surroundings and entertainment, but there was more than a whit of sarcasm in its report. The paintings, concluded the paper, were "appropriate, being an Illinois scene in an Illinois state building."[28]

What really mattered was that the room was finished and that it became a center of much effort and inevitable education. Miss Davis, with her dramatic performance, gave to Macomb a glimpse of the cultural Valhalla never before seen in that town. In the case of "An Evening With Dickens," which she presented in 1907, she led her players to great heights. Achievements such as this could only be matched by such heroic displays as that which occurred when Professor Drake's barn burned with a magnificent display of flame and sparks (Drake's home is now owned by Mrs. Barbara Heap.) *

Even the burning of the barn seemed fitted to time and place. Students and faculty took advantage of the conflagration to hold a gigantic "barn shower," at which one and all ate, and ate, and ate. Truly these would be splendiferous memories for students of those days.[29]

The point has been made that Bayliss had a contented and diligent faculty. One comes to the conclusion that this nirvana was reached through the President's character, and

*Mrs. Heap is presently assistant to the Director of the University Union.

his ability to keep staff members happy. Bayliss worked hard to raise salary levels, and was successful in his aims. Businessmen and bankers in the town were soon persuaded that what was good for each faculty member in this respect was good for them, and they happily gave their assistance to the President.

By the time of Bayliss's death, faculty paychecks were considerably higher than they had been eight years before. One may find in the Board minutes that Professor Hursh was paid $2600 per year, that Dickerson received $2100 per year, and that McGilvrey was paid $2400 per year. One may also find in the same minutes a rather interesting note that a new principal of the training school had been employed at $4000 for the year. His name was Walter Piety Morgan.[30]

Salary was not enough to lead to faculty contentment, however, and Bayliss knew this. He sought to create in Western a respected and honored institution. At a time when most normal schools were afflicted with a superfluity of methodology courses (practically all subjects were taught as such), Bayliss attempted to move along the path of solidity in subject matter.

It is easy to see President Bayliss as a man who firmly believed that good teachers and excellent students were fundamental to greatness in an institution. He further held to the principle that prospective teachers should be "called" to the profession. There should be a dedication of effort akin to religious fervor, and a selflessness similar to that of saints. As Bayliss expressed it: "The children of the children we teach, may teach the forbears (sic) of those whose voices have been destined from the beginning of time to swell the chorus of deliverance. . . ." To this his faculty harkened and followed.[31]

V.

It is difficult to state what might have happened to Western if President Bayliss had not come to such a tragic and premature death. He was an active man, and had never given up the cavalryman's love of horses. The clatter of a horseless carriage on a lonely road in Iowa, and the shying of a nervous horse, brought an end to an era. The crumpled body was carried to the Bayliss farm, and medical aid was summoned. This man, whose sense of duty had dominated his life, could only die by the same code. His last words were those of a boy forty-eight years before, giving his name, regiment, and his division. For the institution which he had governed so well, the effects of this ultimate act would echo down through the years in such a way that the school would never again be the same.[32]

Western's faculty and students were stunned by the tragedy. The institution needed a leader, so the Board quickly gathered and chose John McGilvrey; a man who met the "approval of most, if not all of the other members of the faculty."

McGilvrey was already committed to the presidency of Kent State in Ohio but he agreed to stay on in Macomb for another year. His predecessor, meanwhile, was buried in Oakwood Cemetery in Macomb (twenty years later Hursh was buried in an adjoining plot). Students placed mites into a subscription fund for the purpose of purchasing an organ in his honor. For the next forty years this mighty musical instrument could be heard in the auditorium of Sherman Hall; that is, until it was finally sold during the renovation of the same building.[33]

Soon after Bayliss's death, the man who would eventually take McGilvrey's place was seen stumping about the streets of Macomb. Looking back upon the period prior to World War I, it seems as if Walter Piety Morgan's destiny was the presidency of the Western Illinois Normal School. Yet, as shall be shown, Morgan was in no way similar to Bayliss, and for this reason his accession to power would be significant. Old and respected faculty members were to leave the town; new and ideologically different instructors were to take their places. The character of the school was to change radically from that of the past.

Whatever the causes were for the Morgan revolution, they

broke the Bayliss faculty apart and created a Morgan one. Dickerson went temporarily to Winona State in Minnesota; McGilvrey took Johnson, Dunbar, and others to Kent State; Drake took a position at Emporia State in Kansas; and Susie B. Davis fled to Wisconsin. Thus did the page of history turn from right to left, and into times past.

Chapter III: *Bayliss Wins Out*

1. *Macomb Journal,* June 20, 1942
2. *Courier,* Nov. 15, 1905.
3. *Ibid.,* Mar. 21, 1948.
4. *Ibid.,* June 20, 1906.
5. From a scrapbook of clippings sent to me by Mrs. J. B. Glasgow. The lady employed to take Fairbank's place was Miss Martha Hanna.
6. *Ibid.* Also see *Courier,* June 20, 1906.
7. "Bayliss Memorial Number;" a pamphlet published by school in 1911. Also from a personal communication by O. M. Dickerson.
8. *Proceedings of the Illinois State Teachers Association,* 1911, p. 73.
9. *Ibid.,* p. 77.
10. "Bayliss Memorial Number."
11. *Jackson Collection,* W.I.U.
12. Statement by O. M. Dickerson, Feb., 1961.
13. *Ibid.*
14. *Ibid.*
15. Interview with late Roy Sallee, a longtime instructor at Western. Dickerson later became the president of a school from which, in the 1950's, Western was to employ Dr. A. L. Knoblauch.
16. *Courier,* Jan. 20, 1910, Nov. 20, 1906. Also letter from Mr. Guy Hoyt, Feb., 1961.
17. *Ibid.*
18. Statement by O. M. Dickerson, Feb. 1961; *Courier,* Feb. 14, 1935.
19. *Courier,* Mar. 9, 1916.
20. Statement by Guy Hoyt, Feb., 1961.
21. Dickerson to author, Feb., 1961. *Courier,* Mar. 17, 1932.
22. *Ibid.*
23. *Ibid.*
24. *Board of Trustee's Minutes,* 1911.
25. *Ibid.* Also pamphlet in *Jackson Collection.*
26. Composite picture is drawn by author from many issues of *Sequel* and from personal interviews.

27. *Macomb Journal*, April 13, 1906.

28. *Ibid.*

29. *Jackson Collection.*

30. *Board Minutes*, June 21, 1911.

31. "Dedication Service of the Bayliss Organ," a pamphlet in *Jackson Coll.*

32. *Macomb Journal.*

33. *Macomb Bystander*, Aug. 30, 1911. I have been led to believe that the *Bystander* was published in the building now known as the Lark Theater.

CHAPTER IV

Morgan Takes Command

Some say that before Walter Piety Morgan became the President of Western Illinois State Normal, he had been promised the position by the Board of Trustees. Morgan himself purportedly claimed this, stating that he had been brought to Macomb for the purpose of being "groomed" for the top administrative spot in the school. This may or may not have been so, but if it was, then it was a closely kept secret between Morgan and the Board. Others most certainly fancied themselves as possibilities for the office, and obviously did not know of the existence of such a commitment.[1]

Morgan first came to Macomb during a raging snowstorm on February 26, 1912. As he told it: "I helped break the way from the Hotel Pace to its (Western's) front door early on that morning. I had been invited by President McGilvrey... to come to Macomb for a conference with him about the vacancy which then existed in the headship of the Department of Education and as Director of the Training School." Morgan took the post, but within four months he was named as the President of the school; a change which was to shake the institution from portal to portal.[2]

The chief administrator of Western from 1912 to the early 1940's was born in Vigo County, Indiana, in 1871; the son of William R. and Nancy Piety Morgan. The latter had great influence on the child, for she was not only an ambitious mother

64

but a schoolteacher as well. The father, on the other hand, appears as a rough-hewn farmer involved with the daily prospects of extracting a living from the grudging soil. William Morgan wanted his son to become a farmer as well, but young Walter hated the farm. Years later he would drive his automobile through rural portions of Illinois, and point out to his passengers the hazards of farm life which he had escaped.

What he might not have realized is that his departure from farming was part of a subtle change which took place in America around the turn of the century. Thousands of young people of his day made exactly the same choice; that of leaving the drudgery of the countryside for the more attractive aspects of urban living.

It is remarkable that young Morgan made his choice of a teaching career so early in his life. He was only thirteen when he entered the profession which was to hold him the rest of his life, taking a position in Vigo County which he held for almost ten years. During the summers he went to Indiana State Normal at Terre Haute and won enough credits to be graduated from the two year program in 1895.

This achievement was followed almost immediately by an appointment to a position in the Terre Haute High School; a situation which allowed him to continue undergraduate work at the University of Indiana. In 1900 he was graduated from this institution with a B.A. degree.

In 1908 Morgan moved to Chicago where he began graduate work at the University of Chicago. Here he completed work on the Master of Philosophy degree in 1909, but he stayed at the Midway in order to post more credits in the field of education. It was at this point in his career that he was offered the chance to join the staff of Western Illinois Normal.[3]

An analysis of Morgan's life would not be difficult to make—at least from most aspects. His character was, in essence, tough, resilient, and stubborn. He was a short, heavy-set man, with a pugnacious and determined jaw line. When he walked he leaned against the wind in the same way that he leaned against life. For anyone who was around him for any length of time, it was difficult to think of Morgan as being short. His very nature seemed to give him size.

Part and parcel of it all was the apparent lack of fear which appeared to be a fundamental facet of his inner being. He had a kind of Victorian justification about him which gave whatever happened to be his cause a substance and righteousness. It is doubtful that he ever had qualms about his decisions. He was *always* right, and he *knew* it.

There was a durability about the man too. He had a staying power which confounded those who opposed him. He could not, for instance, admit to being wrong even when proved so. He merely tacked off, like some great ship, in another direction until his detractors were left with only the argument and he with the prize. In this way he could appear to be extremely unthinking. One of his first moves as president, for example, was to peremptorily nip out of existence the budding campus fraternity and sorority life with the claim that it was disruptive of purposeful academic studies.

Yet it is doubtful that there was ever a period in Western's history when there was so much formalism socially speaking. The faculty learned that the holiday festivities at the Morgan house were as inevitable and traditional as the holidays themselves. Students were treated to a liberal dose of formal teas and banquets, the like of which they could never have experienced under the "Greek" system. They responded to them, both faculty and students, because Morgan knew they would, and because he knew that it was best for them.

If one reads the Board notes for 1912, he might reach the conclusion that such formality was implicit and basic in the nature of the man. He wrote to the Board in December of that year, just a few months after his assumption of the presidency:

"We have undertaken to do quite a little for the social life of the students and faculty in the following socials. . . . Faculty Reception, Emersonian Reception, Alumni Banquet at Galesburg, Open Country Club, Platonian reception, Organ recital, Thanksgiving program, Faculty ladies reception, Annual Boys Banquet, Oratorical contest, Christmas program."[4]

It might be gathered from this that his supreme qualities derived from his sense of duty and rectitude, as seen by a Victorian Hoosier. Students soon learned that there was a line which they could never cross; a no-man's land of behavior which he would never tolerate. In the early years of the Morgan administration, the *Courier* took many an occasion to jibe at the faculty both by cartoon and word. Some of these editions were quite outspoken and, according to rumor, the editor would make a serious effort to be out of town on the day after publication of the paper.

Morgan could, by reason of his imperious nature, take only so much of this before he drew the curtain of censorship. When an editor of the same paper complained in 1925 that the lunch hour was too short, the President kept an assembly period overtime twenty minutes as punishment while the editor was publicly chastised. Yet, he was not a man without humor. There was little reaction from him other than laughter when an editor complained in 1919 that Morgan "failed to produce evidence" that he had ever cracked an original joke.[5]

There was much in his way that was good, naturally. While he ordered a standard behavior from his faculty, and would inflict a bitter dressing-down for a violation of any part of it, he stood as the staunchest protector of faculty privilege on the college campus. He demanded for his staff a kind of official respect from the student body unequaled at any other time, and only equaled by the kind of respect he demanded from his faculty for himself. In this way he encouraged his faculty to live a life of rectitudinous character, the bounds of which were set by himself, establishing thusly a pattern for the student body to follow in turn.

Because of the way things are with humanity in general, and because of the way things were in Morgan's time, there were incidents humorously reflective of campus life. Smoking was a habit utterly distasteful to him, and early in his presidency he sought to drive it completely off the campus. As is their wont, however, students found a way, and they did—in closed cars, under dashboards, in secreted spaces in basements, and behind tree trunks.

If smoking tobacco was disgusting, chewing the stuff was even more so in the President's mind. More than one yard man swallowed to the edge of nausea when caught face-on with Morgan while bulging with cud. A faculty member whom Morgan tried constantly to catch in this situation always escaped discovery, for he had developed the art of handling the stuff without creating the need for expectoration. This was exasperating to the President who would engage the man in conversation at times for as long as an hour in order to embarrass him, all without avail. It is little wonder that the *Courier* would parody some well known verse in 1924 in this way:

> For tho from out this bourne of time and place
> My pranks may bear us all.
> I s'pose I'll see our Prexy face to face
> When I have crossed the hall.[6]

Despite his many years as chief executive of the school, it is difficult to search out the innate philosophy of the man. The conclusion is reached in time that he simply thought of his position as one which offered to all the moral and spiritual guidance implied by the office. In order to define Morgan's approach, one must enter into the spirit of the times in which he lived and worked. In 1917, for instance, he argued that a good educational system was one which gave to the "maturing citizen" all that was necessary in "close supervision, direction, and oversight."[7] This is what President Shyrock of Southern Illinois Normal may have felt, or what Livingston Lord of Eastern Illinois Normal might have argued. Morgan was, therefore, in the temper of the times. This was his own blueprint for life:

> A definite aim or purpose; proper mental equipment for both offensive and defensive action; a friendly attitude toward hard work, a desire to master the requisites of some job and do it in the best possible way; loyalty to this job . . . an overwhelming ambition for growth and accomplishment and the unreserved admission that the world owes you nothing excepting return for the effort you exert in solving its problems.[8]

II.

There were few people in Macomb who could have predicted in 1912 the expansion of curricula, student body, and physical facilities which occurred after that date. Morgan took over a small school in every sense of the word at that time and left an institution of some size. Growth was gradual and consistent with normal school growth elsewhere; a fact which leads one to conclude that the same growth would have occurred had any other capable man been president. This inevitable growth, however, served to firm Morgan's position in the presidency, and led to the conclusion in the minds of many that he exacted a powerful influence upon his Board and the State Legislature.

In 1916 the total enrollment for the Normal School and the Academy, the latter the accepted name for the training school during most of Morgan's tenure, was 518. It can only be presumed, since statistics of the period intermingled students of all levels, that the majority of the above figure attended the regular normal school program. One finds also that the Academy had some difficulty in building up its enrollment in the early years.

Five years later, in 1921, Morgan took occasion to point out to the Board that Western had become an important influence in Illinois education. It had handled almost 20,000 enrollments in the eighteen years of its existence, and had graduated 777 students from Normal school courses. In the same year the school registered students from half the counties in Illinois, and from half the states in the Union. Western, so said Morgan, had gained the confidence of school boards everywhere. It had built up a "social, moral, religious, and educational atmosphere," and had made young people "strong and happy."[9]

In 1928, seven years later, the President reported to the Teachers College Board that the school now had 683 college students, of which 489 were girls and only 194 were boys. This imbalance of sexes came principally from the counties of Adams, Fulton, Hancock, McDonough, Rock Island, and Schuyler, indicating that Western's pull was still a regional one. Only in the 1950's and 1960's did this situation change with the influx of students from the suburban areas of Chicago.[10]

The building program inspired by the growth of the student body after 1912 seems to have been quite adequate. Monroe Hall (now Grote), initially conceived by Bayliss, was completed in 1913. This was a handsome structure designed as a girls' dormitory, and it cost the state about $75,000 for the initial appropriation. Monroe, or Grote Hall, became the center of social activities, campus life, and a rigidly controlled study program. "Yes, we get up by bells," said one student of this era, "sleep by bells and go to class by bells. . . ." "Such is bell life in Monroe Hall," she concluded.[11]

By 1916 the campus contained a number of structures— the "main" building, Monroe Hall, the little Academy located to the rear of what is now Sherman, and a set of rambling, ungainly, wooden bleachers rising above the football field. This latter monstrosity lasted until after the end of World War II, and is still remembered by many as an unending source of splinters.

In 1919 a beautiful "fine arts" building was added to the campus; a building designed to house art and music classes. There was an abortive attempt to add a historical museum to the building, and some effort was put forth to collect war relics and other materials. The whole attempt collapsed, and for years students and faculty alike were astonished to uncover gas masks, Moro bolos, and arrowheads; all improvidently put aside in unused cabinets.[12]

Along with the growth in physical facilities came inevitable changes in curriculum and organization. The most remarkable development that occurred in the early Morgan years was the rapid growth of extension classes supported by the college. In 1916 some 523 people in towns and cities throughout the Military Tract were taking courses on the normal school level. Classes from most of Western's fourteen departments found ready acceptance in communities both large and small in the counties surrounding Macomb.[13]

Toward the end of World War I, profound institutional changes took place in the educational structure of Illinois. In a way these were some of the most important developments to affect Western since the establishment of the school. In 1917, under the leadership of Governor Frank Lowden, a new Civil Administrative Code was enacted by the General Assembly. One of its provisions abolished the five separate institutional boards then in existence, and established in their place a single Teachers College Board to be appointed by the governor.

In July of the same year Lowden appointed the new members of the Board, and the freshly created organization proceeded to approve sweeping changes in the five state teachers colleges. In 1921 the name of the Western Illinois State Normal School was changed to that of the Western Illinois State Teachers College. With this change came the right to grant four year degrees, a monumental step in the achievement of some academic prestige for the institution. Shortly thereafter the College granted its first four years degrees to a Mr. Clarence Alton, and to one of its Filipino students, Mr. Cecilio Putong.[14]

These radical changes drew most of the attention of
the community, while more subtle ones relating to faculty
passed quite uneventfully. There was, in the early Morgan
years, a gradual decline in the quality of the staff. An analysis
of the faculty in 1919 shows that while a solitary Ph.D. (in
biology) held an appointment in Macomb, the major portion
of staff appointments were lesser academic degrees. Ten M.A.'s
and four M.S.'s were scattered about the various departments,
and there was one M.Ph. (President Morgan). Five of the
remaining staff taught on the strength of baccalaureates, five
on "special certificates," and seven taught with Normal di-
plomas. It would appear that, although the number of staff
had increased somewhat during Morgan's first years, the quality
at least in academic background did not equal pre-1912 standards.[15]

There were bright lights though, and how well do students remember them? Miss Mabel Corbin and Miss Blenda
Olson, both of the Bayliss period, were held over by Morgan and came in time to exert a fine influence upon great
numbers of Western's students. These two were inseparable
companions, and this is the way most people remember them.
Miss Olson was a handsome Scandinavian type with aquiline
features, and a woman of great activity. Miss Corbin, more de-
mure, taught English and sponsored the *Courier,* and did both
excellently. One alumnus recalls, "She was a truly great woman,
always alert. She truly gave her students something and did not
hesitate to ask them to work. . . . The lives of us all are infinitely
better, I am sure, because this bright, alert, and understanding
little woman came our way."[16]

Miss Jessie Buckner, hitherto undiscussed, was another
Bayliss appointee who was allowed to stay on. She was a
portly woman whose interest in art was not only professional but emotional, and in both ways she sought to inspire

students. One person recalls how he resisted the emotional inspiration of her classes while a student, only to go through a period of abnegation while in Europe years later. "I thought of her many times as we visited the famous art galleries," he wrote. "It is too bad that one must wait a half-century to give credit to a former teacher."[17]

When Miss Buckner died suddenly in 1925, the loss to the school was a sudden one. Her body was allowed to lie in state in the very room in the Fine Arts building in which she taught, while students and faculty alike came to pay respects. It was a rare tribute to her appeal. In genuine sorrow one student wrote: "If I could send the tribute which would express my love for her it would be a bed of purple irises with the sunshine overhead, and the happy sound of bees among the blossoms."[18]

Miss Cora Hamilton remained in the Academy, as did Miss Bessie Cooper. Miss Cooper was a quiet, serene woman who, from some strange quirk of nature, always wore red. When, on occasion, she wore blue instead, the school temporarily went into a state of virtual excitement. Miss Colby stayed likewise, a winsome woman with deep dimples and a broad New England accent. For generations, students under her charge poked gentle fun at her orders that "Marthar" should use more "vanillar."[19]

Robert M. Ginnings stayed on in the Department of Mathematics, an engaging teacher whose fund of stories and jokes was vast but unchanging. Students, years later, cannot recall those harmless little tales individually except by title. There was the "Adam and Eve" joke, the one about "Let 'er go, Gallagher," and a "No price too high" story.[20]

One by one Morgan added people fitted to his kind of normal school approach, however. Oscar Champion came in 1914 as Head of the Department of Commercial Studies, beginning a career which was to carry him through the Office of Registrar as well as that of Business Manager of the school. Wayne Wetzel, the little boy who stood on the edge of the crowd when the cornerstone of Sherman Hall was laid, now having grown up, became an addition to the Manual Arts Department. David Preston Hollis, whose untimely death was to shake the school in 1923, joined the Extension Department; and William Schuppert, soon to be given innumerable sobriquets by his students, assumed the headship of the History Department (this became Social Sciences under President Beu).

Schuppert was an angular man who was afflicted with a slight speech difficulty. The color which he added to the school was soon exceeded, or at least added to, with the addition of Harvey Seal in history.[21] Seal was a bachelor, a plump man when he came to Macomb; a little wizened man when he retired. He was really a timid character who attended virtually every athletic event during his days at Western and these, plus his experiences in the Orient, formed the large portion of his classroom lectures. Since he rarely changed textbooks, he came to know those he did use in exact detail, and could tell his students the page upon which each event was described.

Few people suspected it during his lifetime, but Seal was basically a sentimental man who was caught in the lonely trap of bachelorhood. He would, on occasion, dash off some melody, fit it to some saccharine verse, and then pay to have it printed. One of these songs, "The Little School Mar'm," rather unfortunately came to light some time ago and, after one playing by a willing pianist, was quickly and respectfully buried again.[22]

Schuppert and Seal were decent men, but one can see in them the decline of the importance of liberal arts (or humanities) in the college. It was a sad truth that the history department was in no way the equal to what it had been in 1907. Students knew the pitiful state of this part of their education and, surprisingly enough, so did many of the faculty members in other departments. In other words, the History Department was generally considered "poor" by any standard.

Three of Morgan's more powerful additions were Rupert

Simpkins, Fred Currens (soon to be Ph.D.) , and Dr. Harry Waggoner. Mr. Simpkins was a sincere and logical man who, like Morgan, was a product of Indiana. He became the Director of Teacher Training, and was a great influence upon the lives of many teachers who were graduated from the college.

Dr. Currens was a colorful personality with a shuffling gait and a midwestern twang who took the headship of the Chemistry Department. Later he became the Dean of the College. In the latter position he set some sort of record for running the school without the slightest benefit of obvious organization and routine. Like Abraham Lincoln, he literally carried his papers in his hat and he gave decisions "off the top of his head." Withal, he was a shrewd and perceptive man, deceptively keen in financial matters, and a teacher who was anxious to raise the standards in his own department. His speech was filled with spoonerisms and corn belt phraseology and, before long, his students began to refer to him as "Now S'posen," by reason of his constant use of that phrase.[23]

Harry Waggoner was a special kind of man. He came in 1917 as the Head of the Biology Department at what, for that time, was a fairly excellent salary of $2500. His previous experience had been at Macalester College in Minnesota, an institution which truly regretted losing him.

Waggoner became one of the most popular teachers in Western's seventy years of existence. What made this so was his own bouncy effervescence and love of life, with which students readily identified. His classes were lively discussions filled with learning and they set a kind of excellence which his successors in the field of biology have tried hard to maintain.

Waggoner's great addiction was to golf and, when he took time off from work, he could usually be found out on the course. He was no Sunday golfer though, being a local champion of a sort. Those who played with him remember his almost uncanny ability to put the little white ball exactly where it had to go.[24]

The 1920's brought more changes of importance in the faculty. Death claimed Miss Buckner of the Art Department, and Herbert Bassett of the Geography Department. Bassett, though not feeling well, met his classes on one December day in 1927, only to fall victim to a coronary attack midway through his lecture. Sam Hursh and James Burns continued to fail as the decade rolled on. Hursh resigned in 1925 and died a few years later. Burns held on for a few years, but he died just a few weeks after leaving the college. One must be reminded that, in those days, there was little in the way of a retirement system for teachers; so naturally each individual taught as long as he could before giving up his position.[25]

And still the new teachers came! Walter Eller joined the staff in 1920. Though long retired, he is still an active man in the Macomb community. Mr. Eller was added primarily as a physics instructor but, because of the shortage of staff in the Music Department, he also became the director of the college band. Here affairs were not always easy, for there was no excess of musical talent within the student body. Faculty members therefore filled in to such an extent that the result could scarcely be called a student band. During this period Mr. Eller, along with Mr. Morgan, wrote and published what came to be the college fight song—"We're Marching On."[26]

Mary Bennett, Theresa Wild, and Dr. Clyde Beighey also joined the staff in the 1920's. Miss Bennett had been a student during the Bayliss era and, after having completed much graduate work, returned to the college to join the Biology Department. Miss Wild eventually became the Head of the Music Department, a position which she held until her death in the late 1940's. Beighey, an erudite man and a writer with some financial success, soon became the Head of the Department of Business. He retired in the 1950's, and lived in Macomb until his death in January, 1970.

Little by little, the faculty came to assume the look which it was to hold for two decades more. George Gaylor joined the faculty in 1923 as a permanent member; he had taught at intervals from 1912 whenever he was needed. A further word ought to be said about Gaylor, for among all of the faculty members of his time, he was most likely to willingly cross swords with Morgan. A humorous example of this occurred at Gaylor's retirement when he asked the President to allow him to address a faculty meeting. In a last grand gesture, Gaylor got off his chest some of the rankling thoughts about the administration he had served so well.[27]

Eller, Gaylor, and the rest were soon joined by people such as Dr. Irving Garwood, Roscoe Linder, Harold Schory, Ray Hanson, Rayman Miller, and Miss Margaret Schannenk. Garwood held the first Ph.D. granted by the University of Chicago in American Literature (he insisted upon being called "Doctor"), and he had done some graduate work at Harvard. He was a deceptively strong man, physically speaking, and few in his time realized that he had a good deal of wrestling experience in his background. It may also be added that he was a strong minded man. When he retired in the early 1940's, he did so because his concern with detail had taken a physical toll. Garwood kept busy, however, and lived in the Macomb area for well over another decade.[28]

More will be written about Mr. Ray Hanson later, particularly in relation to Western's athletic program and its growth. Few can argue that he was an influential man in his field. When he became the football coach in 1926, he built a solid backing for the team, and he began several decades of successful competition on the gridiron. It has been said about this quixotic man that his natural ability is such that he would have become a success in almost any field which he might have entered.

It is almost impossible to become angry with Mr. Hanson.

His foibles are his assets; his errors are the magnifications of all human errors. Up to recently he still drove his automobiles at a rapid but erratic clip. His appointments are kept—sometimes—and he still assumes that he knows everyone he meets. He held his position through three college presidencies, and continued to grow in power and influence to his very retirement. He is, indeed, quite a man.

Mr. Linder, who acquired his Ph.D. after his arrival on campus, is a quiet and meticulous man who managed to sustain the extension program through a most trying period in the history of the college. Mr. Schory, on the other hand, was cut from different cloth. He was a clever showman who, as leader of drama activities on campus, brought about an appropriate mixture of Shakespeare, Synge, and Dickens. His Christmas program became a traditional highlight in Western Illinois, and people flocked out of the various hamlets in order to attend them.[29]

Mr. Miller joined the Industrial Arts Department in 1927. He was a kind and conscientious man whose devotion to position and duty was beyond the normal range. His death in the 1950's was premature, even though one could see in his pattern of life an overweening concern with the problems of students, and the details of his post.

Thus was the faculty stabilized. Schuppert, Seal, and others held sway in history; Wetzel and Miller in industrial arts; Gaylor, Simpkins, and others in education; and so on down the line. Throughout these years of the Morgan administration the quality of the faculty varied but little in terms of degrees achieved. In 1925, for instance, there were only three Ph.D.'s out of the fifty or more members of the teaching staff. Twenty-seven of the number had only the baccalaureate or less, with even Caroline Grote falling into this category.[30]

In many other ways were there shades of difference from previous faculties. Since Bayliss there had been a definite decline in the overall quality of the faculty, and there had been a decided change in educational philosophy. Morgan brought to Macomb what was truly a "teachers college" atmosphere, and this in turn killed whatever notions had been entertained to give the school a strong liberal arts approach.

What the President did in this respect may well have indicated his own train of thought, but it also mirrored the prevailing trend in his time. Deweyism and its various interpretations took deep root on Western's campus, and the advocates of methodology were strong indeed. The latter not only ran the school from the top, but infiltrated down into the various departments, either as heads or as more highly paid instructors. Where it was difficult to employ methodologists, such as in history or English, the tendency was to bring in individuals who would at least be sympathetic to the field of pedagogy. Schuppert, one would assume, was a good example; while Garwood, it was argued by some, had passed through over a dozen institutions of higher learning before settling into the receptive character of Western. In many ways Morgan's approach hurt the school, for in the 1950's, when it became possible to move toward a true university status, Western was unable to overcome the strong teacher training influences which had dominated it in the past.[31]

III.

Walter P. Morgan was a man whose approach to problems was to meet them in their incipiency. If, by chance, they did arise, then his next tactic was to override them.

In a sense, he was faced with such difficulties in the first months of his administration with the Bayliss faculty. The change from the diplomatic and slow moving Bayliss to the dynamic and strong Morgan was too much for some of the teaching staff to take. Others were disappointed at not having been considered for the presidency, and still others just wished to move.

In view of the number of years which have passed since that time, it is almost too difficult to fathom the depth of the dispute between the new President and his faculty in 1913; but, whatever it was, Morgan won. His victory was the result of his almost incomparable ability to get along with his Board, and his grim determination to succeed. Not that he didn't have his disquieting moments. A letter from Morgan to a friend illustrates this. "You can do much to quiet the alarm," he wrote. "I think any extraordinary action . . . would do much to put our institution in an unfavorable light before the public. . . ." In the end, the unruly elements recognized Morgan's preeminence and, as has been pointed out, a new faculty came.[32]

No sooner had these developments subsided than others arose. The spark at Sarajevo flared up into international conflagration, and soon Europe was at war. The *Lusitania* went down, the Black Tom explosion tore up Jersey City, more ships went down, and soon the United States entered World War I. For Western, and for Morgan, it was temporarily a moment of emotional exuberance and permanently one of sober recollection. One *Courier* in 1917 reported that the chapel period of the previous week was given over to a "pageant of nations" in which the patriotic songs and flags of the Allies were presented. Another "pageant", given a few months later, produced an "impressive spectacle." It carried "out the idea of struggles through which the world had gone thus far in obtaining Democracy and also prophesying that militarism would be crushed by Democracy, aided by Truth, Justice, Love, and Hope."

These were the necessary accoutrements of national conflict; the whipping up of emotional fervor.

Week after week in chapel the students got liberal doses of "patriotism." A study of lectures in the auditorium in 1917 included such topics as "The Americans in the World Crisis," "The Threat of German World Politics," and "American Interest in Popular Government Abroad." Even President Morgan found himself constrained to speak on "Democracy, the Basis of World Order." These were the things which a whole generation, led by F. Scott Fitzgerald, would ridicule and mock a decade later.[33]

Soon the boys went off to war. Some wrote home of an entirely new world far removed from Western Illinois. One soldier boy found time to write to the *Courier* that he had just visited New York and, while there, had seen Al Jolson in "Sinbad" playing at the Hippodrome. Dazzled by it all he went back to Broadway on succeeding nights to see the great Irish tenor John McCormack, and Mr. and Mrs. Charles Coburn. It is little wonder that one of the popular songs of the era asked how the boys could be kept on the farm—after they had seen Paris.[34]

On the home front, and at Western, people worked and waited. Male students virtually disappeared from the campus, and girls energetically joined the Red Cross. Gold stars were sorrowfully noted by Miss Mabel Corbin who, more than any other faculty member, took the times to her emotional heart. Professor Bassett of the Geography Department went to Washington to do special work, and other male members of the faculty created a "home guard." Girls were inspired by exhortation to write to the boys in uniform, a task which really required no encouragement; and students were called upon to raise money for the "French War Orphan Fund."

As one might suspect, prices went sky-high in Macomb and students were among the first to complain. And uniformed young soldiers came home on leave to find themselves eulogized in ways which left them embarrassed. Wounded men, such as a Canadian soldier who has lost his arm at Vimy Ridge, came to Macomb to help raise war bond sales, and patriotic festivals were held on campus in which soldiers from nearby army posts were drilled on public display.

So it went! The campus Y.M.C.A. industriously packed boxes for alumni serving overseas, and faculty wives worked long hours making candy to send to former students now in the service. It was a different time and a colorful one. It is little wonder that the *Courier* could say: "We can make ourselves most healthy, the most efficient, the most intelligent and wide-awake person that lies within our power, and then when our country calls us we will be prepared."[35]

The war ended, and most of the boys came home. Some came back to finish their schooling in Macomb, some never did, but in the end the conflict was an event which faded into the past only reluctantly. For the next decade it remained as a landmark by which one could say it was "before" or "after" that such and such an occurrence took place.

Beyond the routine-shattering events of the war, and the influenza epidemic which followed the great conflict, a kind of placidity settled over the campus which was broken only by an occasional faculty misfortune, a visiting speaker, or sprig of gossip passed along from person to person. The faculty taught and Morgan administered; the school grew but gradually; and a successive string of Republican governors brought no drastic revolutions to the Macomb campus.

Socially, and this was true to a large extent of the Morgan period, the faculty maintained a more than discreet distance from town society, preferring to regard itself as one happy family which partied together at the slightest pretext. This, apparently, was what Morgan desired, and in some cases insisted upon. If a young couple, new to the faculty, hesitated about entertaining, then Morgan entered the picture and proffered some presidential advice. Silverware and china were lent to the couple, or one should say delivered to their doorstep, and a party took place. Bridge was the preferred medium about which a gathering was held.

The wall of reserve built between town and gown by such activities served both to help and hinder the school. Some considerable respect for the faculty emerged during the Morgan period, but so also did some resentment. A strong-willed President saw little need to react to such problems however, and his faculty followed in turn.[36]

Chapter IV: *Morgan Takes Command*

1. Personal interview with Mr. Morgan before his death.

2. *Courier,* Sept. 23, 1927.

3. Collection of newspaper clippings given to me by Miss Lauretta Robinson, formerly an instructor in the training school.

4. *Minutes of the Board of Trustees,* Dec. 5, 1912. I have drawn Morgan's character from the recollections of many people associated with him, and from my own experience with him.

5. *Courier,* Jan. 24, 1919. *W.I.S.C. Bulletin,* 1952-1953. On one occasion the flag became stuck half-way up the flagpole. Morgan gave a hand-over-hand report to an assembly meeting in the auditorium while a young boy climbed up to loosen it.

6. *Courier,* Jan. 11, 1924. There are many people who, for some reason, pridefully remember being caught by Morgan while smoking. Even to this day I wouldn't print the name of the faculty member who chewed tobacco in Morgan's presence.

7. *Macomb Journal,* Dec. 19, 1917.

8. *Ibid.,* June 5, 1916.

9. *Normal School Board Proceedings,* July 1 to June 30, 1921. *Courier,* April 18, 1921.

10. *Board Proceedings,* Sept., 1928.

11. *Sequel,* 1917, p. 114. *The Military Tract: Normal School Quarterly,* June, 1914.

12. I recall seeing these items when I came to Western. They eventually disappeared; one supposes into the hands of antique "collectors."

13. *Courier,* Sept. 30, 1915.

14. *Board Proceedings,* July 1, 1917 to June 30, 1921; *President's Annual Report,* 1946-1947.

15. *Board Proceedings,* 1917 to 1921, plus my own personal observations.

16. Statement by Mr. Ralph Bishop, Feb. 28, 1961.

17. Statement by Mr. Guy Hoyt. Feb., 1961.

18. *Courier,* May 13, 1925. It is difficult for contemporary students to comprehend the close relationships between students and faculty years ago. O. M. Dickerson, for instance, corresponded with two of his former students for sixty years.

19. Mrs. Martha McLean Davis to Miss Susan Davies, April 27, 1961.

20. *Sequel,* 1917.

21. *Courier,* Feb. 1926; *Sequel,* 1924.

22. I have a copy of this song.

23. *Sequel,* 1917. I knew Dr. Currens very well.

24. *Board Proceedings,* through period 1917 to 1921.

25. Interview with Mr. Walter Eller.

26. Mr. Eller again.

27. When Gaylor pressed Morgan too closely in faculty meetings, the President generally dismissed the meeting. Much information about Gaylor comes from Dr. Marcy Bodine, formerly Head of the Social Science Department, and a man who knew Gaylor well.

28. *Courier,* Feb. 24, 1927.

29. *Board Minutes,* Sept., 1926.

30. *Sequel,* 1925.

31. Many members of Bayliss's faculty became nationally famous. The same could not be said about Morgan's faculty, which was strongly oriented to teacher training.

32. Morgan to C. W. Flack, May 23, 1913, *Presidents' Collection.* It is hard to get those who know to commit themselves on the events of 1913. Only two interviewees were willing to make strong statements on the faculty changes of the time, and they did not wish to be quoted. *Board Minutes,* 1913, hint at Morgan's problems with the Bayliss faculty.

33. *Courier,* April 12, May 11, Dec. 14, 1917. From what I have read, the faculty was much more active in the war effort of 1917 than in World War II. Perhaps there were reasons for this; for example, the heavy extension loads carried by the staff from 1941 to 1945.

34. *Ibid.,* May 30, 1919.

35. *Ibid.,* Nov. 23, 1917. Clippings given to me by Miss Corbin, whom I personally knew, and by Miss Lauretta Robinson.

36. The story about the silverware and china was told to by a faculty wife, now deceased. There is no question about the admiration of Dr. Morgan by townspeople. Most agree that there would be no student unrest on any campus administered by such a man as Dr. Morgan; the students *wouldn't dare.*

CHAPTER V

The Morgan Era: Phase II

The "roaring twenties" were wonderful years for the nation, and for all of those Americans who were prosperous enough and young enough to enjoy them. The country took the scandals of the Harding years in stride, overlooked the activities of big city gangsters, watched with pride the conquest of the Atlantic by Lindbergh, and viewed with mixed emotions the emergence of the "miniskirt" of the pre-depression years.

Few middle class Americans could doubt the claims by some big business leaders that the country had reached the permanent plateau of prosperity. Despite the rambling cynicism of Sinclair Lewis and H. L. Mencken (he once thought that sixty college presidents should commit suicide) , the tycoons of the business world had obtained an aura of sanctity. All that one had to do to buttress any lagging faith in the dictum that "the business of government was business" was to read the best seller of the era, *The Man Nobody Knows*, by Bruce Barton. Here Christ was compared to a big business executive; the head of a board of directors consisting of the Apostles.

Some men could see solitary but persistent clouds on the horizon, however. Bernard Baruch noted the gathering surpluses in warehouses and the declining freight-loadings of railroads, retrenched his financial empire, and waited for the storm to come. Another, the father of a future president of the United States, sold short on the exchange, and went home to await the catastrophe. Others in 1928 did not see, and took President-elect Hoover's campaign speeches on the invulnerability of the American economic system to heart.

For the Western Illinois State Teachers College, the next fourteen years were to be filled with problems both large and small. First came the depression and then lean years, and then Hitler and the growing threat of war. Beginning in 1929, first one and then the other were to create for President Morgan a series of problems which were to make his last decade in the presidency of Western a hectic one.

The rapid faculty growth which had occurred in the early years of the Morgan administration ended abruptly with the onset of the great depression. It is true that, in the period between the national election of 1928 and the beginning of the economic crisis, there were some additions to the staff; but these came to an end in 1933. After that time there were only replacements, plus a very occasional new position allotted by the Teachers College Board. The proof of the lessened growth lies in the number of faculty positions in 1930, which was seventy-one, and the comparison to the number of positions in 1941, which was eighty-five.[1] Some growth, it was true, but it was painfully slow.

The most interesting development during the 1930's was in the number of doctorates added to the staff. The fact was that the degree had become a necessity to the ambitious college instructor; a "union card" to promotion and pay increases so to speak. As noted previously, there were only three Ph.D.'s on the staff in 1920; by 1941 there were approximately twenty-eight. Two of the latter were honorary (they were also honored by the Board), which left twenty-six of the earned variety.[2]

Despite these changes, Western remained essentially a teachers college with all the connotations which that term implies. The so-called arts areas were staffed by a good many people holding an education or methodology degree of some kind and, though they may have been the most excellent of instructors, their approach to their work was conditioned by their training.

For this reason, from the standpoint of pure talent the Education Department, which had acquired the larger number of doctorates, stood out. Other departments, carrying individuals with education backgrounds or people who had terminated their education with the master's degree, gave little support to contentions pushed at sister institutions that the teachers colleges must eventually become universities.[3]

This is not to say that the quality of instruction throughout the school was weak or unusual for the type of institution which Western was in 1930 or 1940. Biology, for example, did have in it individuals who had doctorates or who had pushed their work towards the final degree by research.

For most of the faculty holding master's degrees though, this represented the terminal degree and they did no further work. Frankly, this was a factor which did not enhance the reputation of the institution, no matter how well it fulfilled its purpose as a teachers college. Other schools in the state which operated under the Teachers College Board acted to remedy the situation by employing only people who had been granted the doctorate, or who were well on their way to it. A study of Southern Illinois Normal University in 1941 reveals almost twice as many doctorates as Western; and Eastern Illinois Normal became during the 1930's a kind of model institution for having a high percentage of doctorates on the staff.[4]

Time took care of this problem, of course. As the years rolled by, the older faculty retired and individuals holding advanced degrees were brought in. Caroline Grote and E. E. Van Cleve finally left the campus in the mid-1930's, both having served through a great period of growth. When Miss Grote came to Western, for example, the student enrollment was around two hundred. At the end of her career, there were over a thousand in attendance.

One final note on Miss Grote, and the tides of time and change. When she died in 1941 at the age of seventy-eight years, her passing was barely noted on the last page of the college newspaper. One is reminded of Dr. Louis Schleier's widely quoted comment about retirement. Few people really remember, he used to say: one's leaving a school is comparable to a rock thrown in a pool. There is agitation, the ripples ring out from the point of impact, and gradually disappear until there is nothing left.[5]

The year 1928 brought a new group of eager young faculty to Macomb. These included such names as Bessie Myers in English, Theodora Pottle in the Art Department, Dr. Arthur Tillman in the Geography Department, Dwight Bailey in the Education Department, and Mr. Waldo Horrabin and Paul Neuriter in the Chemistry Department. The last named is recorded here because he was a brilliant young man who held a doctorate from the University of Vienna, and who was a fine addition to the college. Unfortunately, as in the case of other fine young additions to the staff in the 1930's, he did not stay. When times got better, as they did, he left for greener pastures.

Dr. Tillman served a long stint as the Head of the Geography Department until the late 1950's, entering at that time into what most of his colleagues and students regarded as a regrettably early retirement. He was a steady teacher who regarded high scholarship as an accomplishable goal at Western, and so imbued his staff with this philosophy. Bailey, likewise, had his following. He came to Western as a rural education specialist, and finished his career at almost the same time as the demise of that field of study in the institution.[6]

Mr. Horrabin is a man who deserves a special kind of description. Perhaps no other person serving on the faculty today, or in the past, has been so identified with the school as this man, lest it be Mr. Wayne Wetzel, formerly of the Industrial Arts Department. He came to the institution in the 1920's as a student, and created such an impression that at the first opportunity President Morgan added him to the training school staff. For years he taught his subject there in a manner which few students of those times can forget. It is not easy to make chemistry an interesting subject for all students, but in some mysterious way he was able to do it.

Soon there were other faculty additions. Edwin Schreiber, a genial and learned man, joined the Mathematics Department in 1929; and in the year immediately following there came to the campus Miss Velna Sollars, Miss Jennette Terrill, and Dr. Louis Schleier and Dr. Julian Archer in the Education Department.

Schleier was a big robust man whose geniality was a facade for an intensity which it seems that few people came to know. He taught in a broad and sweeping style and accepted entirely the principles of Dewey and Kilpatrick. The latter point is accounted for by the fact of his doctorate from Teachers College, Columbia University, and a long teaching career which carried him through normal schools in Washington and Montana as well as the Education Department of the City College of New York. Eventually he became the Director of Graduate Studies at Western, a division of the school which grew rapidly until his death in the mid-1950's.

Dr. Archer was a sanguine man whose character contrasted greatly from that of Schleier's. He came from West Virginia, and his path towards the doctorate brought him through such institutions as Ohio University, Columbia University, and New York University. Few students who attended his classes will ever forget him, for while attendance to sessions with other instructors might become routine, they never did with Archer. He was an extremely agile man, intellectually speaking, and students had difficulty in keeping up with him. Archer eventually became the Dean of Graduate Studies, a position which he filled with the same diligence which he demonstrated in his classroom work, and with the same conscientiousness which he showed towards life in general. He died in 1964, and the position which he had held was filled by Dr. Henry Sather.[7]

Dr. Moses N. Thisted, who occupied the position of Dean of Men for many years, came in 1932, as did Dr. Hilda Watters, an extremely popular instructor in the social sciences. The likeable Miss Sarah Miner, later Head of the Home Economics Department, came in 1936. So did Dr. Kathleen Brophy who rose to the headship of the Women's Physical Education Department. Miss Juna Reynolds also came in the same year to adorn the English Department. She is now retired. And finally, one of the appointments to the Academy in the same period was Dr. Clifford Julstrom. Dr. Julstrom, later Chairman of the Music Department, is an accomplished Swede from Iowa who has led his staff to solid achievements in the field. It may be said that there are few high schools in the western part of Illinois which do not have a band director trained at Western, a women's physical education director not influenced by Dr. Brophy, or a home economics instructor not counseled by Miss Miner.

The closing years of the 1930's saw the addition to the faculty of Dr. Glenn Ayre in mathematics, Miss Lyndall Swofford to the library staff, Marjorie Burke and Kent Pease to the training school, Dr. Marcy Bodine to the History Department, Dr. Grace Sproull to foreign languages, and Mr. C. W. Garner to the Men's Physical Education Department. One of Morgan's last appointments, made on the eve of World War II, was Mr. Allan Laflin to the Business Education Department.

Dr. Ayre is a tall slender man who rose from a position in the training school to the headship of the Mathematics Department. Later, during the late 1950's, he was appointed Dean of the School of Arts and Sciences.

Dean Ayre, now retired, speaks with a southern Illinois ring to his voice, and one arrives at the opinion that his roots, or at least his affections, are still in that part of the state. His education took him to Southern Illinois University and to George Peabody College; the latter school the source of his doctorate.[8]

Dr. Sproull, now retired, was a kindly and able teacher whose influence for good in the college was greater than most might imagine. She has a clever and incisive mind, and is quite adept at arriving at the heart of any issue under argument. As the Head of the Department of Foreign Languages in the 1950's and 1960's, she fought to enlarge this area of study against the apathy of the times.

There are few people in Western Illinois who do not know Dr. Marcy G. Bodine. He is a genial man whose energy impresses those who come into contact with him. Few places in the world have been closed to his ubiquitous nature, as his record in the travel study program denotes. Shortly after President Morgan's resignation, Dr. Bodine became the Head of the Department of Social Science and, despite great difficulties, created a department which commanded the respect of the college as well as the surrounding areas served by it.

One could not possibly detail all of Morgan's appointments to the faculty. There were many who were excellent people but whose stay in Macomb was short-lived. There were still others, a few, whose names ought not to be mentioned. Morgan, like most presidents, came to regret employing certain teachers through the years. One, for instance, was a very poor instructor, but Morgan could not remove him because of misfortune in the person's family. There was another individual who wore his pajamas to class under his trousers; yet Morgan kept him on. There were others, brilliant people whom Morgan might have desired to keep, who could not accept the tightly knit society which the President had organized. These people left for what they thought were greater opportunities.

It does appear obvious that the quality of the Morgan

faculty improved during the 1930's. The cause may have been the far-reaching effects of the depression. Nevertheless, the teaching staff retained the Morgan imprint; it was a teachers college faculty with a pedagogical approach. The latest educational doctrine out of Teachers College at Columbia was passed on to Macomb, and it gained adherents. There was an increasing trend in the college towards vocationalism, and a greater and greater emphasis upon the art of teaching rather than upon sciences and the arts. This approach was perhaps best illustrated by Dr. Louis Schleier of the Education Department who once stated that teachers were "human engineers" who should teach people rather than subject matter.[9]

III.

As the 1920's rushed to a close, it seemed obvious to those who had closely observed the Illinois educational scene that the state had neglected the development of the teachers college. The concept that a college education was a necessary adjunct to a high school degree was now gaining some acceptance and the growing popularity of teachers college courses placed a burden on the five teacher training institutions.

Just prior to the depression, when the country seemed to be in an everlasting state of prosperity, the old normal schools of Illinois began to receive some belated attention. In 1927 Morgan, in concert with the other normal school presidents, opened the bid for appropriations by pointing to certain obvious problems. Western was in a crowded condition, Morgan said; it needed at least six new instructors in order to bring classes down to manageable levels. There was a need for a new training school building, for children had to "recite" in basements. Last, but not least, the faculty needed a six percent pay increase.[10]

Western did receive a new training school, now known as Simpkins Hall, but it came through the Public Works Administration, a federal agency. Unfortunately Western achieved little success with its other requests, however, for the depression served to turn the public's attention elsewhere.

Yet, to a great extent, the effect of the economic catastrophe upon this institution was less than on other state colleges or private schools. Morgan had been a conservative man in his requests and, when the depression hit, Western was really understaffed rather than overstaffed. No faculty members were released on account of the lack of funding. Morgan had been conservative also in advancing salaries of his faculty and, in 1929, Western's staff probably lagged behind our other institutions in this respect. Consequently the cuts in faculty salaries in succeeding years were only minimal.[11]

An examination of faculty income at the height of the depression would show a rather amazing contradiction, and that is that the economic situation of the teaching staff really improved. The lack of substantial salary cuts, and the increasing deflation of the dollar accounted for this. One must remember that in 1934 there were many talented people who worked on federal relief projects for forty dollars a month. High school teachers in many areas received pay warrants rather than actual cash. There were, according to federal calculations, some fifteen million people unemployed in the country, and millions more only partly employed. Yet, in the same year, deans at Western drew the steady income of around $3700 a year, professors about $3400, associates around $2700 a year, and so on down the line. One must also be reminded that this was, in most cases, pay for only nine months work. Summer work brought extra income.[12]

In a sense then, the main problem centered about the students—how to get them and how to keep them. If one examines the muster rolls for the thirties, it is obvious that there was great difficulty in the first of these problems; that of keeping the enrollment up. It is difficult to compute college enrollment for the time, for teachers college presidents had strange ways of reporting to their boards on this phase of college life. Yet it appears that Western's student body numbered around 950 in 1934, a decline of about forty from the previous year. Persuading high school students to come to Western became, therefore, somewhat of an accepted practice with the school. In 1937 a unique institution called "guest day" was begun for this purpose. On these occasions high school students were invited to visit the campus, to visit classes in session, and to observe functions of the college.[13]

The fact that Morgan was able to maintain his staff in the face of declining enrollments was somewhat of a miracle. In 1935 there were only 869 students, marking a further drop from the previous year. Of these, about 220 were working for the National Youth Administration, doing odd jobs about campus in exchange for small amounts of money. For these young people life was most certainly far removed from that which students enjoy today. There were virtually no students who drove cars, except commuters, and few were allowed the luxury of marriage.

Virtually all students worked in some way—in restaurants, in those factories still operating, or for the school. Student activities, as shall be pointed out later, became quite purposeful, for these young men and women really *wanted* to go to college. As Morgan put it in a statement to the Board in 1933: "Many of our students seem especially in need of funds this year.... Many of our students are doing lighthousekeeping, including several groups of boys."[14]

Another aspect of the depression was the drastic change in student aspirations. Jobs were only open to the technically skilled, and for this reason students adjusted their programs to vocational areas. English as a major field, for example, fell to six percent of the student body; mathematics dropped to less than five percent; and physics majors totaled only slightly more than two percent of the student body. Home economics, on the other hand, showed great increases, and on registration days long lines formed before the tables of that department. This area now had over eleven percent of student majors. Commerce also became popular, rising to over fourteen percent. This subject still remains as one of the largest major fields chosen by students at Western.[15]

In 1937 Morgan had reached the twenty-fifth year of his administration in Macomb. The year became a turning point in the history of school; not because the event was celebrated at the Hotel Lamoine around the theme "Apples of Gold in Pictures of Silver,"[16] but because for external reasons the problems of the faculty and student body drastically changed. The depression was still present but in a milder form. Now, however, the thoughts of most young people were filled with the growing prospect of military conflict. It is true that, like many students of the time, these young men and women felt that Europe was far removed, and that any conflict there could be avoided. Even after Hitler invaded Poland in 1939 most Western students thought that the United States could and should stay out of the affair (hadn't Professor Schuppert so predicted in his history class?).[17]

The first week of December in 1941 seemed like a normal one for that time of the year. The weather was holding fairly well, and the winter snows had not yet come. The *Courier* gave its calendar of coming events. There would be a lecture by some imported housing expert on "How America Lives." The Kosmopolitan Klub, a social science organization, had a discussion on the effects of the European war on the United States. Up in the auditorium students were practicing on a play to be presented at Christmas called the "Good Shepherd."[18]

Thus it was when war came a second time to Western's campus. Morgan, one year away from retirement, reminded his student charges that calm and understanding were necessary in the new crisis. It was not long, however, before casualties of war made their presence felt. Soon the campus was wrapped in gloom; and already some alumni had become gold stars. Dean Moses Thisted put on his uniform and left for extended duty; and Coach Ray Hanson, that sprightly soul, put on his beloved Marine green and said goodbye.

For Morgan himself, the last years of his administration were difficult indeed. He became very ill, almost mortally so, with some people saying that the illness came from the thought of having to leave the institution rather than from the onset of age. The ailment, which was fortunately overcome, probably had its origin in both. The road had been long and hard for the man, and the feeling that the Board had been somewhat inconsiderate concerning him probably aggravated his emotions.[19]

When he finally turned his office over to his successor, he could look with some satisfaction on the years which he had served. The *American Association of Teachers Colleges,* an organization which Morgan was instrumental in establishing, rated Western as Class A, and almost everywhere the institution was regarded as a sound teachers college. A 1940 study showed that its graduates could be found in every state of the Union but five, and in seven foreign countries. Altogether, since its founding, there were about 3500 graduates from the school, most of them going into the teaching profession.[20]

Morgan's later years had been a fairly happy time; that is, for the faculty. This body was, in reality, a community within a community and there were, as one old-timer nostalgically recalls, no "empire builders." There were virtually no faculty responsibilities in decision making, for Morgan made them all.

Yet there were some who looked to Morgan's successor as a person who might relax regulations and restrictions upon campus life. They abhorred the necessary bridge parties, and the Christmas teas. The same people failed to understand that Morgan was a product of his time and that change was inevitable. Presidents come and go. Some grow in spirit to the last day of their duties, while others do not. Fortunately the fates had arranged Walter Piety Morgan's retirement at the shifting of the wind.[21]

IV.

Housing, as in the case of other facilities and phases of school life, has undergone changes of great importance. Western's beginning was based mainly upon householders' cooperation which, until the economic advantages of renting were determined, was singularly lacking. Once it was discovered that money could be made from keeping students, the community responded.

In the early years, students were completely at the mercy of financial circumstance. If they came to Macomb with resources, they were then able to obtain substantial rooming places; if they were short on money, then they were forced to scramble in order to survive.

Most rooming houses were large rambling structures located on Adams or Sherman streets. They were poorly ventilated, and lighted in some cases with oil lamps. Many of the rooms were bleak and bare, and furnished with whatever the householder might find at local auctions. There were instances in which the housekeeper violated every possible principle by bunking many students in a single room. In still others, both girls and boys were allowed to rent in the same house.

Most often, students of the early days preferred to cook for themselves. Consequently the cooking, bathing, sleeping, and studying facilities were normally part of the same rooming space. For this same reason it was not uncommon for householders to improve some former stable so that it might be used for renting purposes. From this situation there developed student "clubs," nothing less than communal arrangements, in which individuals pooled their resources and talents in order to meet financial needs.

During the first five years of the institution, housing conditions were indeed quite poor. In 1906 the school authorities found conditions which were shocking. There were over forty rooming houses which accommodated students. Eighteen of these places allowed both sexes to live within the same house. Thirty allowed cooking privileges, with the facilities for such within the individual sleeping rooms. None of the rooming houses had single beds. Six houses had inside toilets, the remainder being equipped with the outside variety. Only ten had central heating, while the rest were heated by stoves. Students' rooms were generally unheated.

There were still many homes in 1906 which used kerosene lamps, while still others were lighted with gas jets. None of the houses provided laundry or ironing facilities, which left the student to carry out those tasks within his or her own quarters.

The growth of the school in following years continued the increased demand upon housing in Macomb. In 1909 a second survey was initiated, and it showed that there was still considerable room for improvement. Now there were sixty householders in the city. Twenty of these allowed light housekeeping privileges under restrictions established by the school authorities. Twenty-four of the rooming houses had inside bathrooms, and most allowed hot water at least once a week. Twenty-four, or slightly more than one-third, had central heating; one house still used kerosene lamps; and fifteen allowed some laundry work and ironing at an additional cost to the roomer.

By 1911, the school began to take a firmer control of the troubled housing situation by demanding of householders that they conform to certain restrictions. President Bayliss pressed rooming house owners to provide more of the modern conveniences of indoor plumbing, central heating, hot water, and better lighting, as well as improved furnishing of rooms. He further asked that parlor privileges be allowed to students so that they might not feel imprisoned within their rooms. He also insisted that rooming places for women be "approved" by the Dean of Women, though the men could live anywhere they so desired.

It was not until 1928 or 1929 that a third housing survey was completed. The full extent of the school's insistence upon better housing conditions is shown in the results. The cost of a room at this time, one year before the depression, averaged slightly over two dollars a week, while board approximated five dollars a week.

There were some one hundred and forty householders within the city. Thirty-three of them provided board for the students, seventy others allowed light housekeeping, and twelve allowed student cooking in the family kitchen. Twenty-five of the number provided a separate room for eating, all but three of the houses had central heating and inside toilets, while one householder still did not provide an inside bathroom. Fifty of the householders provided towels for their roomers, ninety allowed laundry and pressing privileges for extra remuneration, and thirty maintained a piano for use by students.

At this time the school authorities established even stronger restrictions upon householders. They were enjoined to enforce regular study hours, limit social functions controlled by students to the weekends, restrict the time of "gentlemen" callers, keep close regulation on the activities of women students, and to keep their houses "hygienically" clean. Girls were to be sent to bed no later than ten o'clock, except for one "sit-up" per week for study purposes.

As indicated elsewhere, the completion of Monroe Hall played an important part in changing student housing conditions in Macomb. Not only did it tend to set standards for social behavior within the student body, but it stabilized costs and quality of furnishing among the private householders. The *Macomb Daily Bystander* reported in 1914 that Monroe Hall would become a standard for all with its approximate price of four dollars per room per week.* Meals were priced at three dollars per week, and each room was fitted with a "tungsten" light, a table, two rockers, two rugs, a dresser, a chiffonier, an iron bed, a lavatory, and several closets.

The great depression in the 1930's had a certain effect upon housing conditions. The enforcement of previously established rules upon householders was generally set aside, for many poverty-stricken students were forced by circumstances to live in most unfortunate situations. Householders, furthermore, could rarely afford the upkeep sometimes necessary to maintain houses in their former condition. Consequently many young men and women were housed in dank basements or attic rooms, and often worked off the cost of such quarters by performing tasks for their housekeepers.[22]

V.

The faculty meeting as an instrument of procedure in the American college has likewise undergone the inevitable adjustment to time. Western provides no exception to this course of events, for the faculty meeting in this school, once an important aspect of campus life, has virtually disappeared from the scene today.

During the early years of Henninger and Bayliss such gatherings were informal conclaves, almost of a social nature, at which issues both large and small were discussed. Faculty members made known a point of view, and in some cases these presidents took the advisements as a matter of policy. In many instances matters of a campus concern such as problems of registration or the contents of the catalog became the subjects of ridiculously long arguments and sometimes resulted in hurt feelings and outraged sensibilities.

---

*The four dollars was for room and board. It was possible for outsiders to take board only at three dollars a week.

During Bayliss's time there was less of this because of the President's fine ability to ameliorate and compromise. He had a way with him about these problems, which he considered mountains made from molehills. There was, on one occasion, a long faculty debate on whether football as a competitive sport should be abolished. This was part of a national reaction against the activity, there having been a number of deaths, and a considerable scandal connected with recruiting.

Bayliss allowed his faculty to argue the merits of both sides for some time, and then pointed out that there was really nothing to discuss. The school could not have a football team for there was nobody who really wanted to take on the added burden of coaching the team. When one young man, Dr. Oliver M. Dickerson, arose to defend the sport, Bayliss then stated that the institution had found a coach, Dickerson, and that the school could now field a team.

The faculty meeting in the Morgan period took on an entirely different coloration. This President saw the gathering as a means of forcing his faculty to share the responsibility of decision making. For Morgan's faculty, the decision was generally made first by the President, and then presented to the faculty for approval. Usually some discussion followed with the President's judgment always prevailing.

It may be added that Morgan's concept of agenda included the most trivial letter arriving at his office from a book company or the slightest indiscretion of a wayward student. For this reason his program was quite long, usually beginning in mid-afternoon, and proceeding well beyond the dinner hour.

Many faculty members sought for excuses to miss such gatherings. Morgan, however, had a photographic memory of the assembled group (roll was also taken) and usually made a point of mentioning the absentee teacher's name, or of calling him to his office for a reprimand. One, for example, always arranged to have his secretary enter the meeting room shortly after the beginning of the session with the message that he had a long distance telephone call. This worked successfully for a number of occasions until the President finally caught the significance of the secretary's appearance. Still others attended, and found methods by which they could dream the long hours away. It was not that such meetings were tension-ridden, as they would be in later times. It was simply that they were tedious and boring.[23]

The faculty meeting began to change radically under succeeding presidents. President Frank A. Beu held to the monthly pattern of meetings which existed when he became president, but saw the meeting as an information dispersing device. On these occasions the faculty was told of latest developments with respect to the state budget, new rules concerning curriculum, or different regulations pertaining to campus procedure. In the latter respect staff members were often informed as to grass reseeding in certain areas (they should not walk upon the grass), or that the light bill had been much too high and all care should be taken to turn off lights either while using the classroom or when leaving the room.

Usually at each faculty meeting the group was informed as to current athletic events, and the prospects concerning victory or defeat. The time given to such meetings varied considerably, for on occasion they would end after five or ten minutes; on others a longer time would elapse. There was a like variance with respect to the temper of such meetings. At times there would be hilarity; on other occasions there would be considerable tension.[24]

During President A. L. Knoblauch's administration, the faculty meeting was held but once a term. There were special or extra meetings, especially during times when issues of special concern arose. At both regular or special sessions, the faculty tended to polarize into two groups; the A.A.U.P. or arts and sciences faculty, and the anti-A.A.U.P. or vocational schools faculty.

President Knoblauch's approach to the faculty meeting was a casual one. He left an impression with some that he didn't really care for large meetings involving intricate discussion. Yet he was easy in his approach, and often directed discussion along the line of banter and exchange. There were times when this was quite good; there were other times when dissident faculty members felt that issues were not squarely faced.

President Knoblauch continued the tradition of introducing new faculty members at the first meeting of the year; that is, until additions became too numerous to detail. This was a harrowing moment for the younger novices to college instruction, for they felt the general scrutiny of several hundred of their older colleagues. It would have been well for the newcomers to have known that they were not being viewed too closely, that the veteran faculty members were present only because of custom, and that most individuals present were ready to leave the meeting at the first opportunity.

Faculty government, as indicated by the gradual decline in faculty meetings, likewise underwent certain changes during the administration of Dr. Knoblauch. It might be pointed out that real faculty power had always been limited at Western. This was not unusual through the years, for in most institutions the boards of trustees made policy. Presidents, particularly at Western, occasionally delegated some responsibility to the faculty in policy direction, but rarely the authority.

Under the Morgan administration there were many committees, but the real subjects of interest to the faculty—salary, curriculum, etc.—remained strictly in presidential hands. Salary, during the years following 1912, was determined by President Morgan through a combination of factors. Students were polled for their opinions of various teachers and these results, plus the President's own opinion, brought an individual decision by

Morgan on each individual staff member. In view of current cries for student evaluations, it might be interesting to note that most faculty members of the 1920's and 1930's decried this business of student sampling with the argument that it led to lower standards. Teachers, said many on the Western staff, tended to pander to student tastes rather than to teach objectively and dispassionately.

Morgan's administration was undoubtedly an authoritarian one. Most faculty members of the period thought so, for the President came to faculty meetings with the Business Manager, Oscar Champion, on one side, and the Registrar, Miss Hertha Voss, on the other; and with most decisions already made.

In the late 1930's, however, a significant development in faculty government began to occur. Under a relentless hammering by his critics, and perhaps haunted by thoughts of his impending retirement, Morgan relented in his practices. There appeared the first written constitutional outline for faculty government, *The Faculty Handbook, 1939-1940*. This thin pamphlet detailed much in the way of rules, regulations, and the powers of certain committees. A suggested "flunk" percentage was given, holidays were listed, and so were advices on faculty attitudes. One sees in the publication the laconic hand of the Dean of the College, Fred Currens, for on one page is listed a general instruction to the teaching staff on faculty business. It is, simply put, "keeping it a secret."

The *Handbook* was not without value however. A significant step was taken to bring Western up to the levels of faculty control achieved previously at Southern Illinois Normal University and at Illinois State Normal. It was stated: "Any matter which any faculty member considers worthy to be presented to the faculty for action, may be so presented by filing it with the President at least one week in advance." It was further indicated that faculty decisions on such matters would prevail.[25]

Though the *Handbook* was not the first step in faculty government, it was the first real one at Western. Shortly thereafter many of the liberal instructors became concerned should the seedling of faculty participation fall into the hands of an unsympathetic future president. To meet their arguments Morgan appointed a committee to work towards codifying existing policy and to search for new concepts of governance. Dr. Louis Schleier chaired this group, and the result of their labors was the so-called "red book." The most important innovation here was the establishment of a Faculty Council to aid in advising the president. The balance of power remained relatively unchanged, however, for most of the members of the Council were to be appointed by the chief administrative officer.

It was this growing framework of government which the new President, Frank A. Beu, found at his inauguration. He readily constructed his policy around it, however, and the "red book" continued to operate until the early 1950's. At that point, the growing ineffectiveness of some committees, plus the active discontent of some faculty members over the imbalance present in the Council, led to a rewriting of the constitution.

Dr. Grace Sproull was appointed to head the new committee which consisted of such people as William Lipsey, Dr. Paul Blackford, Mr. Waldo Horrabin, and Dr. Victor Hicken. The result of their labors was the "green book;" red was an unpopular color, according to one of the committee members. The constitution produced was essentially a revision of the previous book with some vital changes. For the first time elected members would outnumber appointed ones.[26]

With the resignation of Dr. Beu, and the appointment of Dr. Knoblauch to the presidency, the days of the "green book" were numbered. The large number of new administrative deans, plus new schools in the university, necessitated another constitutional revision. Dr. Harriet Stull chaired the new committee which produced, after much discussion, a broad revision of the previous structure of faculty government. The Council was dismantled, and a Senate created. Much power of appointment was returned to the president, particularly with respect to committees as well as the Senate. The results of several years of operation under this newer constitution showed a constant weakening of real faculty participation in decision making. Voting on almost every issue illustrated a consistent two-to-one margin in favor of the administrative viewpoint.

With the election of Dr. John T. Bernhard to the presidency, a third revision of the faculty constitution has taken place. In it there is an attempt to create a true "Faculty" Senate (the previous one had many non-teaching administrators on it), and a definite commitment by the administration to full faculty participation. The document as now produced consists of fifteen single-spaced typewritten pages, and is detailed with regard to committee responsibility. Only time will tell whether the new constitution will succeed in solving the tangled problem of administrative responsibility and faculty aspirations.

If it is solved once and for all, it must be realized that the ultimate solution was not achieved overnight. The victory was won by seventy years of dedicated faculty effort; in some cases, by the loss of promotions, tenure, or raises of not a few dedicated instructors. Newcomers to the campus should realize this, and recognize the sacrifices of the past.

Chapter V: *The Morgan Era: Phase Two*

1. *Open Gate and Open Door,* a leaflet put out by Western Illinois State Teachers College, 1930. Also *Sequel,* 1941.

2. *Sequel,* 1940, 1941. My own tabulation.

3. Southern Illinois Normal had many more doctorates on its faculty, for example.

4. My own tabulation.

5. *Courier,* Sept. 17, 1941. Schleier's comment was part of the first conversation I had with the man.

6. *Board Proceedings,* Sept. 1928.

7. *Courier,* Sept. 13, 1939.

8. I owe my information concerning these faculty additions to a general survey of the *Courier* files.

9. *Ibid.,* Nov. 19, 1931. These comments come from an address by Schleier.

10. "President Morgan's Report to the Board," April 25, 1927, *Board Proceedings,* 1925-1929. The last building added before the depression was Morgan Gymnasium, now called Brophy Hall.

11. I owe my information to several retired faculty members.

12. *Board Proceedings,* 1934.

13. *Ibid.* Guest Day remained as a college tradition until a little over a decade ago. There was a carnival-like atmosphere present, with each department attempting some sort of display.

14. *Board Proceedings,* 1933.

15. *Courier,* Nov. 2, 1939.

16. Material in possession of this writer.

17. *Courier,* Nov. 15, 1939.

18. General study of the *Courier.*

19. Interviews with several faculty members of this period.

20. *Courier,* Feb. 28, 1940.

21. The remark concerning "empire builders" was made by a long-time faculty member.

22. I owe much to Miss Susan Davies, former graduate assistant in Social Science, who researched some of this material.

23. The picture I have drawn here comes from interviews with Morgan era faculty members. The faculty member who used the telephone trick should be recognizable.

24. My own recollections.

25. *Faculty Handbook, 1939-1940.*

26. I served on this committee. The suggestion that red was an improper color came from an individual who was much concerned about the activities of Senator Joseph McCarthy at this time.

CHAPTER VI

The Students

The most overused phrase in the 1960's was the "generation gap." According to those who were inclined to expound upon it, the generation gap included, among many of its postulates, the notion that there was a broadening misunderstanding between youth and their elders. According to some, the older generation had become too complacent, too obsessed with materialism, and too much rewarded with affluence. Only the younger people, so said these spokesmen, understood the needs of the time.

Those who tried to reason did so with generous applications of history and fact. True, there was a war in Viet Nam, but college youngsters, provided they maintained their grades, were not drafted. The college students of the 1960's probably had more automobiles, more money, and better college facilities than any generation in history. There was no depression, said the middle-aged American of the 1960's, and the war in Viet Nam was used only as an excuse by youth for sit-ins and rebellion.

One cannot write the real story about an age until time casts a perspective upon it. The probable truth is that the generation gap notion is vastly overblown, and that youth has always strained at the bonds of discipline. The rebellious youngster of one decade is the struggling and somewhat frantic middle-aged American of the next. The middle-aged ultra revolutionary only becomes outrageously dated, and as much a part of the gap between the ages of man as his conservative counterpart. Was it not true that Jeremy Bentham, at the turn of the Napoleonic era, was a liberal because he espoused the notion that the least government was the best government? Thus it is that times, habits, customs, and beliefs change. So it has been at Western.

In the brochures and pamphlets broadcast by Western Illinois Normal in 1902, there were stated some of the conditions of entrance into the institution. Evidence of scholarship in the form of a "teacher's certificate" or high school diploma was required, and the student should be of proper age. The applicant was to be of good "Moral Character," though no real definition of these qualities was given. It can be presumed that the term applied to such behavior as gambling, smoking, drinking, and loose ways with the opposite sex.[1]

What Western enrolled in the way of students in 1902 was what it has taken in during most of its history. The earliest students were normal and average products of the middle or lower middle classes; students who were ordinarily well-behaved, but who occasionally broke the traces and misbehaved.

As Mr. Henninger was to find out, no school administrator can expect perfect behavior from his students; not all of the time, and not in the United States. The first president was forced to suspend a young girl in the very first month of his administration for "profane language and unladylike conduct." In the following year another student, a young man, was sent home for hitting one of his fellows. Henninger was also to find out that he was not always able to act so freely. Shortly after the young man's expulsion he received a letter from the lad's mother: the boy was really not bad, she said; he was a sensitive youth who needed understanding, and furthermore the boy's uncle who was on the "normal school board" would be shocked to hear of his expulsion.[2]

Thus was it not uncommon for such events to occur. In 1905, on West Carroll Street, second year students engaged in a brawl with freshman normal school students over the possession of school colors tied to a lamp post.[3] In the same period the *Courier,* commenting on student behavior, complained: "If gum-chewing, dropping books, whispering, nudging one another, and all such foolish actions were eliminated, everyone would consider chapel a pleasure and profit." The same paper also had comment some years later on further aspects of student behavior:

> "There are some who persist in throwing erasers out of the windows or at their neighbours; and some have not yet been able to curb their instinct for whittling and marking desk corners or throwing ink on the floor. Then, worst of all, so far as actual damage is concerned, a desk top is occasionally burst off its hinges or a chain broken down. Then, on the outside, when it is wet, there are a few who are so rushed they must cut the corner and go across the grass.[4]

These digressions were committed by few students, the greater proportion being on good behavior. After all, being caught straying from the accepted mode of behavior had its punishments, and the code set down by the early administrations of the school was strict. One alumnus remembers that it was a time of no "flunk slips," permits, or "admits" to class. Recalcitrant students were simply sent to the president for long lectures or punishment. Girls were required to be very modest in dress and when, on one occasion, a woman student entered the library with sleeves rolled up, the librarian asked her to withdraw until she returned properly dressed. Men students just didn't enter the same quarters vestless or coatless.[5]

Yet life was not dull, even for those who hewed the line of good behavior. It was a light time, and a gay one, and life was filled with much that was good. There were always the picnics in fair weather, held on the banks of the Lamoine

River or in the "ravine." In the cold weather, when the first snows had fallen, student groups hired horses from the local livery stables and rode bobsleds and sleighs over the hills west of the campus.

On special occasions such parties would sleighride all the way to Colchester on a "moonlight night" with the "air just keen and cold enough," warm up with oyster stew at an inn in that mining town, and then return home singing as they rode.

Too, there was skating in winter, and swimming in the summer. It wasn't always easy to find a body of water suitable for the latter activity, and it was common for students to defy the edicts of the various presidents, and swim in Lake Ruth at night. This persisted to some degree until President Morgan issued an order to his night watchman that all clothes found near that pond would be confiscated on the spot.[6]

One notable characteristic about this early time was the tendency of the young people to socialize in large groups across sexual lines. It was common for one house full of girls to entertain boys from a neighboring rooming house, and to be paid back in turn. It was comparatively easy to do this, for there was always popcorn to serve, fruit punch, or pancakes to cook in colder weather. Dancing, not acceptable to the early administrations, could be carried on behind pulled blinds and to the tinny blare of the "graphophone." There was always plenty to talk about—studies, the faculty, and food; and, when the conversation ran out, one could still return to eating. A good picture of such young people was drawn by the *Sequel* in 1905:

> The Junior boy was bright, to be sure, and alive to his opportunities, in some respects almost equal to the Senior . . . his strong points were clog-dancing and music. The Junior boy was affected; he made many vows, and was much given to pleading. . . . The Junior girl, however, was a young lady of many attainments. . . . Sometimes she wore her hair *a la pompadour,* sometimes *a la pancake.* . . . In brief, she was good looking, a good cook, a

good mixer, good student, with pugilistic tendencies, and was usually a Methodist.[7]

The opening of Monroe Hall in 1914 added a new fillip to campus life. Here, President Morgan hoped, could be centered the social activities of both students and faculty, a development calculated to create an atmosphere of a girl's finishing school within that building. From the beginning the girls who lived here were limited in terms of behavior, particularly in relationships with the opposite sex (an old joke among the girls was "Does Monroe Hall live here?"). Girls were to be quiet and orderly, the hall regulations stated. Permission had to be obtained from the housemother in order to attend church, school entertainments, night lectures, music programs, and weekend picture shows. The study hours, for two hours during the evening, called for all girls to be in their rooms. One night a week girls could sit up one hour later for study and, concluded the regulations, "gentlemen" could call on weekend nights but could stay no longer than ten o'clock.[8]

Living in Monroe Hall was, in those days, a delight and a privilege to Western's women students. It was a way of life not to be found in a solitary room in a boarding house, or in a basement apartment on Adams Street. There were approximately ninety-eight other young ladies to talk with, as well as the kindly Miss Grote who acted as housemother. All meals were planned ahead by the staff, and when they became dull, the large electric ice cream freezer was put to use.

Since the building was a sort of no-man's land, it came as a shock when, after scheduling a home economics class in the Hall, fifteen men signed up for the course. Much to the delight of ninety-nine girls these favored few were taught the mysteries of raising dough and making cookies.[9]

Among the other aspects of behavior and morality, Western students mirrored the pattern of the era in which they lived. In the early days it was not easy to break the moral code, for, since the girls were guarded quite closely, one had to work rather hard to step outside the bounds of propriety. Furthermore, each student attended chapel, where he listened to moral lectures designed to brace him to the straight and narrow.

Occasionally a young couple might manage a venture to the local amusement park, at which they could slide down an incline in a boat and into a pool of water, or they could attend the Gem or Princess theaters in order to see a Mable Normand two reeler.[10]

If dating was discouraged, it was considered infinitely more daring to allow one's self to be "picked up" by any young man fortunate enough to own an auto. This was true into the 1920's, as is attested to by one alumna:

> Walking uptown on a Saturday night in summer was an adventure in running a gauntlet of Model T Fords. The drivers and their companions—young men from the country around Macomb would call "How about going for a ride—why not save father's shoe leather. . . ." Any girl tempted to accept the offer knew it meant suspension if she were caught.[11]

Smoking among men students was certainly frowned upon, but among the girls it was generally considered an indelible sign of sinfulness. If a girl was seen smoking, even by her friends, it provided conversation for the entire term. Older women who had acquired the habit, perhaps older teachers attending summer classes at Western, found it difficult to find a time and a place for a cigarette. One woman walked mysteriously into the ravine behind Grote Hall every day at the same time, and upon her return could be seen "taking some white tablets." It was feared by some that the school had a drug addict on its hands until it was affirmed that the white tablets were mints to cover smoker's breath.[12]

In the 1930's it was customary for students, both men and women, to hide in parked autos about the campus in order to smoke. Cigarettes were lighted under dashboards while at least one in each party watched for the omnipresent Morgan. Discovery meant expulsion. Under President Beu, however, smoking regulations were sensibly relaxed along with restrictions on other forms of behavior.

Drinking, rarely a problem in the early years, became a minor bane of American college life in the 1920's. Offenders were not as numerous as "flaming twenties" literature has led most to believe, but there was still enough to attract some public attention. In fact, the *Courier* of 1925 drew the conclusion that the white-hot decade was nothing more than a smoking cinder; investigation at Harvard, it said, had concluded that "half" the student body was "bone dry." Though the *Courier* made no statement about the other half of Harvard's students it did say: "there is little opportunity for dissipation at the college. Prices of liquor as a rule are too high for the majority of students to indulge in drinking."[13]

This was the decade in which the Eighteenth Amendment forbad the making and sale of liquor throughout the Union. The *Courier,* by self-admission, had indicated that hard liquors or beer could be bought in Macomb if one knew the outlets. The fact of the matter was that Macomb and Western were little different than the rest of the nation. The "great experiment," as statesman had called it, was destined to failure from the beginning. For that singular figure, President Morgan, it was not only a legality however; it was moral law. He was determined to shelter most of his students, if not all, from the deletorious effects of alcohol.

If it was true that Morgan's wrath was that of Jupiter when confronted with any liquor problems, it was even more true that he regarded sex with ultimate Victorianism. While there may have been a breakdown of high moral codes at other colleges, Morgan held the line against the changing times.

It was probably so that an occasional Western coed was sent home *enceinte* but that situation occurred only rarely.

Even in the 1930's, when Victorianism was a fading illusion, Morgan enforced a strict code of behavior both upon his students and faculty. When a psychology professor gave a test on attitudes among his students at Western, he found that "lower moral standards" existed in the eastern schools, that half of the men would adopt the religion of their wife, and that seventy-five percent of the men would marry a wife of lesser intelligence and education. The real fact of the matter probably was that students who wanted to ramble freely upon the green did not come to Western, and that the college attracted girls and boys from more restricted moral backgrounds.[14]

With the coming of President Beu there was a general tendency to relax the rigidity of the past, and to accept the facts of the times. Smoking became permitted within the campus grounds, though President Beu properly warned students of the health hazards involved. Drinking (prohibition now over) was recognized as an insolvable problem, although Dr. Beu never accepted it as proper whether indulged in by faculty or students.

With the return of the veterans from World War II there was a further retreat before the concepts of the times. When Dr. Beu indicated in a national magazine that there were "no sex problems on our campus either during the war or since," he was probably speaking in a relative sense.[15] Times had changed, and college students had changed with them. As the *Courier* noted in 1954: "It seems as though the modern day student to be modern must master the ability of smoking a pack a day, drinking too much, being careless in morals and ethics, and generally wasting his time in college."[16]

During the 1960's, as will be pointed out below, there came a revolution in attitudes towards sex; a revolution which was to be found everywhere. Older couples who visited the campus were somewhat shocked to see the open behavior of couples outside of the dormitories. What had happened partially was that "necking" had moved from the porch swings of rooming-houses to the outdoor environs of the high-rise dorms. There was less modesty about it all, to be sure, but even Morgan, during his day, had difficulties in regulating the normal passions of young students. In 1940 the *Courier* complained: "Even the art of osculation can be studied at first hand with various couples more than willing to demonstrate to the student body at large, just how such a most skillful and necessary craft may be carried out." "After all," concluded the paper, "there is a time and place for everything."[17]

III.

The reasons why students through the years have chosen Western as the college they wished to attend are almost as varied as the species of trees on the Western campus.

Students came to Western in past years for such reasons as the low cost of teacher training, the nearness of Macomb to their homes, the advice of relatives or Normal alumni, the possibility of earning part of the cost of their education, or the attractions listed by the school in pamphlets, circulars, or catalogs.[18] One suspects that many come to Western today because of the relatively low cost involved.

In the early days, it was assumed by Henninger and Bayliss that, since Western's students came from a lower economic class, social training must be an inevitable part of the school's educational system. As it was expressed by one of the early educators at Western, the social life of the school should "compare favorably with the fashionable boarding school."[19]

Convincing the students that culture was important to them was not an easy task, even sixty years ago. It was not even easy to get some of the students to come to class on time, as the *Courier* pointed out. Tardiness was a disease of the campus, said the newspaper, and "heroic means should be taken to break up the habit, even to locking the doors at the beginning of the recitation."[20]

Grammatical usage took a terrible beating from the young students of earlier days and, as indicated in some quarters, "has went," "I done;" and "don't" for "doesn't" were common errors in speech and writing.

Nor was it easy to arouse in most the contemplation of beauty in commonplace things. "Take your field glasses and bird book, nothing else, and spend an afternoon out on Crooked Creek," urged the college newspaper in 1917. "Beauty is every-where and forever present; we merely need eyes that see and ears that hear."[21]

Faculty members made heroic attempts to lift the general cultural outlook of these willing young students. The latter were divided into groups and assigned to faculty homes as guests at meals. Many alumni, still alive, remember Professor Garwood's "forest of Arden," with roasted suckling pig, and the rigid formality of it all.[22] A solid attempt was made by some of the earlier administrations to guide students to good lodging places which would provide "moral, social and cultural" ad-vantages above those present in the small towns from which they came.[23]

In the 1920's a vigorous attempt was launched to encour-age Western's students to read books not necessarily required in the classroom. The library in 1915 placed the best sellers of the time upon display in the hopes of lifting the general cultural outlook of the campus, mostly without success. The exception to the rule, the student who did read, meant a kind of triumph, however. In the 1920's another venture of this sort was tried, and not a few students found pleasure in reading such books as Lindbergh's *We*, or Harold Bell Wright's *God and the Grocery Man*.

Other popular writers of the 1920's included Edna Ferber, John Galsworthy, Zane Grey, Oliver Curwood, and Edward Bok. Magazines read by the Western student body included the

American, Cosmopolitan, Saturday Evening Post, Harper's, The Literary Digest, and *College Humor.*[24] None of these publications were extraordinary journals—note the lack of journals of profundity—but then Western did not have extraordinary students.

It is quite possible that today's students, about whom more will be written later, are not too different from their predecessors. A survey taken today might indicate some reading of Gore Vidal or Truman Capote, or of *Life* (it has pictures), *Time, Playboy* (it has pictures), and *Sports Illustrated.* A judgment of Western students made about forty years ago might well be applicable today. "The average student," the *Courier* said in 1925, "is too self-complacent. He does not consider that there might be a possibility for him to develop a new trend of thinking or that maybe his experience is not broad enough to justify him a judgment on every question."[25]

Yet these faults are perhaps the results of the values of present society. Not so long ago the University advised incoming students to walk with an "air of pride" and an "easy stride." "Wise employers," it stated, "refuse to have a person around who does not 'pull with the team'—no matter how brilliant he may be individually, because business is truly an affair of reciprocity."[26]

IV.

A significant boost to intellectual ferment on the campus was given by the returning war veterans of 1945 and 1946. These young men had seen a good deal of the world and of humanity in general, and it was difficult for them to accept what was obviously poor teaching or outmoded formulas. These people lived, in many cases, in poverty, and struggled to raise families within the limits of the "G.I." check.

The necessities of life sometimes forced them to bring children to class with them; the mother being ill or at work.

Invariably the men worked part of each day in local factories; a condition which made it quite difficult for them to keep up their studies.

Their apartments were makeshift, one being described as consisting of packing boxes or barrels for furniture, towels for table cloths, and calendars for decoration. One veteran, after fixing his quarters in this manner, embellished them with, of all things, a statue of Mozart.[27]

They deplored old regulations, and yet were torn with the desire to anchor their lives upon the bedrock of formality. "Let us start some new traditions," one naively proclaimed in 1950.[28] They viewed their college from a far different aspect from their professors, some of whom suffered from a kind of professional myopia. One veteran described the "new college" as one in which there was some kind of answer for every problem. If a slow reader found difficulty in passing his courses, he should consult a reading specialist. If the student couldn't study properly, he should read a booklet on how to study. If he was unable to keep his grade percentage up to requirements, he should be counseled properly.

When the number of veterans began to decline in 1948 the institution missed their drive. As the Courier expressed it: "We have a lot to thank them for both the past and for what they are doing for Western."[29]

One characteristic of the great depression and of the postwar years was the working student. Since 1932 Western has accepted this condition as an important factor in the college community, and many young students have earned all or part of their way through school and to graduation. Attempts by students to make ends meet were supplemented by food supplies brought from home, or by actually living at home on weekends. One source indicated in 1943 that almost every student carried food from home after the weekend and, in 1950, President Beu indicated that forty-seven percent of the student body migrated to their homes on Friday. In the same 1950 report some forty-eight percent of 585 men students answering the questionnaire admitted to doing outside work. Out of 419 women students participating in the same survey, one-third indicated that they were earning part of their own way.[30]

The employment of students in various industries about Macomb—the pottery or porcelain plants, as examples—was a part of a significant social change on Western's campus. Family responsibilities brought this about for many students, plus the desire to acquire a car or to simply pay one's way through school. Marriage in the college community was mostly of post-war vintage. In the early days it was a rare occurrence and, even then, it was the result of a long and tenuous courtship. There was some jest and yet depth of meaning in the headline of a *Courier* in 1929. "Post doubts allayed," the paper announced, "union consummated."[31]

As in the case of marriage, there has been a like change in dating as an aspect of courtship. To be sure, there was some dating in the early days but the intensity of relationship so common in the 1950's was most certainly not present then. Boys and girls studied together as a part of the courtship procedure on campus, they attended movie shows, or they dated for the infrequent dances held on campus after 1919. The depression days cut into this behavioral pattern rather severely so that the low budget coke-and-dance date became the accepted thing. Many alumni of this period remember some little dancing spot on West Jackson Street to which a couple could go for a soft drink and, by exercising a willingness to wait for coins to be placed in the juke box, they could dance all evening.

After 1939 there was a marked change in the philosophical and moral pattern of the Western student, for a war was clearly in the making for the United States and this became a source of deep concern to most young men in Macomb. As the *Courier* put it: "It doesn't take brains to shoot a gun nor intelligence to pick a quarrel. . . . We want peace! Millions for defense but not one man for tribute!"[32]

War began, however, and with it came a loosening of old attitudes and approaches. Eventually most of the young men left the campus for military service, but on their occasional return dating and all that went with it showed the effect of the conflict. For the girls who were left in Macomb during these war years, life seemed dull and somewhat meaningless. More than one alumna recalls the tedium of the times, broken only by an occasional visit by a lecturer to the campus, a movie down at the Lamoine starring Kay Kyser or El Brendel, or a dance to which panting young soldiers from nearby Camp Ellis were brought.

The end of the war amplified the breaks in the old pattern of behavior, and with them came heavy and prolonged dating as a prelude to marriage. The average date in 1947 involved two young people who had been going together since their high school days. The girl wore a dress stretching to four inches below the knee, and with a two inch wide belt at the waist. She also wore angora anklets and brown loafers, along with a hooded raincoat. The boy was usually dressed in indifferent trousers with a colorful sports jacket. In his pocket he carried $2.34 (the cost of an average date), and with it he took his girl to a movie, a basketball game, the skating rink, or to a weekend hop (free and sponsored by a campus organization). The end to the evening was one kiss, or many, by the couple in the ravine, a spot so located that it afforded protection from the prying eyes of the night watchman. Supposedly the girl then returned to her lodgings in conformance with hours regulations.[33]

As will be shown below in a discussion of the 1960's, dating has undergone further changes from those incurred in the 1950's. Generally, however, it seems as if the contemporary college student has far more pocket money than the student of ten years ago, and that more cars are owned by today's students. Morality, so the magazines tell us, has undergone another "revolution," but that does not seem to be a new development. At any rate, it must be remembered that the picture of any period is set by the most outrageous or extreme elements of the society of that era. The "flaming twenties" were not flaming; the "fabulous fifties," looking back, were not so fabulous; and a decade from now, one may view the 1960's as rather sedate. The extreme behavior of some students today will soon become part of the fuzzy past, somewhat like the hip flasks of the 1920's, or the goldfish eaters of the 1930's.

V.

Arthur Schlesinger, Sr., in describing campus life at the turn of the century, wrote: "Virtually every institution also had a numerous array of literary, oratorical, musical and dramatic societies, often, like the fraternities, bearing Greek names though lacking in their exclusiveness." Oratory, he said, was significantly more important as an intercollegiate function than athletics, and had been so since the initial debate between Harvard and Yale in 1889.[34]

Western fitted itself to this pattern, and held to it for at least the first twenty years of its existence. Two oratorical societies were organized in the beginning, the Platonians and the Emersonians, and each student on campus was compelled to join one or the other.

As the *Clionian* reported in 1905, the activities of both groups occasionally spilled out beyond the confines of oratory. The Platonians, it said, not only debated on the issue of the efficacy of labor unions, but were entertained by a reading called "The Traveling Parson." The Emersonians, on the other hand, presented a quartet which sang "The Lost Chord." "After searching all over the stage and under the piano," complained the editor, "the members of the singing group found a large enough portion of the 'Lost Chord' to enable them to continue."[35]

Rivalry between the two groups was very intense. Contests in debating were a matter of course, but it also became acceptable for one to play pranks upon the other. Firecrackers or noxious bombs thrown into meetings held by the two groups were not uncommon occurrences. It was all part of college life at the time, however, and virtually every student who endured the Platonians or Emersonians remembers these societies with affection.

By 1920 the effectiveness of both societies began to fade. The call of the local movie was much more enticing than a discussion of the Treaty of Versailles.[36] Yet both the Platonians and Emersonians continued to struggle on until after the end of World War II, and on to 1948. In 1949 the English Department finally administered the *coup de grace* by uniting both societies into the Canterbury Club.

There were other activities in the early years besides the literary societies. The orchestra was organized in 1905 with a Mr. Burch, a faculty member, as the director. Burch left the following year, however, and Mr. P. V. Olker of Macomb took over the leadership of the organization, and expanded its size and offerings.

The *Clionian*, previously noted as the forerunner to the *Courier*, was the first newspaper for the school, and within two years the Normal had its own yearbook in the *Sequel*. The name of the latter publication purportedly comes from Shakespeare's *A Comedy of Errors:* "Oh! let me say no more: gather the sequel from what went before."[37]

Contemporary with the Emersonians and Platonians was the formation of a Y.M.C.A. chapter on the campus. Through two world wars and a depression, this fine organization offered services to the ordinary student; services which were not assumed by any other group.

Drama clubs made an inevitable appearance on campus in the early years. By 1941 most plays were performed in the open air theater in the ravine. Townspeople were invited to watch the performances as well as students. In the 1920's there was a movement to unite all of the theatrical efforts into one group; the idea being that superior performances would result. The aims were achieved for the college drama society performed James Barrie's *Quality Street,* Tarkington's *The Trysting Place,* and Synge's *Riders to the Sea*; all done superbly.[38]

The practice of bringing outside talent to the campus began early. The Coburn Players performed in 1916 and 1921. Carl Sandburg, who had been raised forty miles away, came to the campus in the 1920's. Lorado Taft, the famous sculptor, visited Western in 1929. There were many others: Albert Spalding, the violinist; Wilfred Grenfell, the explorer; Lew Sarett, the poet; Harry Elmer Barnes, the historian and social scientist; and Amelia Earhart, were among them. Though attendance was rarely compulsory, the auditorium was generally filled by students and townspeople who were anxious to see and hear individuals as important and famous as these.[39]

As the student body and faculty grew, an attempted simulation of larger schools was natural. By 1913 there were two fraternities and two sororities. Morgan disliked these organizations, however, and virtually drove them out of existence. Other organizations were encouraged in their stead and, in 1919, Morgan began to allow these groups to hold dances on the campus. It was not that he liked dancing, as he reported to the Board, but it was just that the student pressure to indulge in this activity was too great and he had to give way.

The Monroe Hall girls sponsored dances every other Friday night during the 1920's, and other organizations held dances at specific times. Some of these affairs were intricately formal and traditional, particularly the class dances, and they present in retrospect a lovely picture of the past. With no small amount of nostalgia can students of the mid-1920's recall the Christmas dance of 1925, with the mistletoe and holly, the big snow which fell that night, and the carefree temper of the times.[40]

The organizational aspects of campus life continued to grow under President Morgan until, by 1927, there were some thirty-seven student groups on the campus. Though these included agriculture clubs, music clubs, *ad infinitum*, the list continued to increase and by 1941, just before the war, there were forty-one such campus activities, big and little, active and inactive. The absence of the young men in the ensuing years and the drastic changes in social life in the same period brought a fortunate end to most of them.

The retirement of Morgan, and the beginning of the presidency of Dr. Beu, brought a return of the "Greek" letter organization to the college. Dr. Beu, it seems, supported such groups and, while he guarded their reputations carefully, he appeared to encourage their growth. By 1944 there were a number of these organizations including Phi Sigma Epsilon (it was organized in 1910 but was killed by Morgan in 1913), Sigma Tau Gamma, Alpha Sigma Gamma, Alpha Sigma Alpha, and Pi Kappa Sigma. The postwar years brought great activity among these fraternal and sororal associations, creating a situation in which the campus was dominated by the so-called "Greek" student. By 1953 there were nine groups on the campus, and in 1956 there were eleven fraternities and sororities at Western. All in all, there were fifty-three different student organizations in the college.[41]

It is most difficult to discern the role of the student organizations at Western today. There seems to be little activity in the old departmental associations such as the Canterbury Club or the Kosmopolitan Klub; the latter an old social science society. The old social club, wrapped about a hobby or major field, seems to have disappeared as a factor on the campus. The reason probably lies in the fact that neither the faculty nor the students have the time for such associations.

The modern student appears to be more sophisticated than his predecessor of a decade ago. He may or may not join a fraternity, but when he does, it is to be suspected that his emotional attachments are not as strong as his father's were in the previous generation. The competition for his time, the disintegration of the old faculty-student relationship, the pressure of school, problems of the military draft, and other factors tend to splinter each student's loyalties into many parts.

VI.

When Dr. A. L. Knoblauch was formally installed as the President of Western Illinois University in 1959, a new era began. The elaborate ceremony, with representation from 115 colleges and scholarly associations, went far beyond any previous ritual of this type. A sumptuous dinner was prepared for the guests, and each was presented with an ashtray formed in the shape of the state of Illinois. The school had come a long way from President Morgan who had frowned on smoking anywhere on campus.

President Arthur L. Knoblauch was the ninth president of the school; the previous leaders being Henninger, Hursh (interim), Bayliss, McGilvrey (interim), Morgan, Beu, William Lipsey (interim), and Richard Browne (interim). The newest chief administrator was as unlike the rest as Henninger had been to Bayliss, or as Dr. Beu had been to Morgan. More will be written about Dr. Knoblauch later, but it may suffice to say that he is a well disciplined man, he dislikes smoking and drinking, and he has a delightful and charming wife who surely has helped her husband's career in the area of administration.

With the advent of Dr. Knoblauch, there was no abrupt

change in the behavior or conduct of the student body at Western. There was, in the beginning, considerable talk about lifting standards in the University, for there had been some criticism previously in that respect. In general, however, the pattern relating to entrance requirements and grading followed the pattern of the entire American educational system. By 1961 the *Courier* was running letters or articles complaining about the numbers of failing students in the institution; the cause being laid, as usual, upon one or two of the major departments.

By 1960 the first of the so-called "beatnik" (later called "vietnik" by some) appeared on campus. Seal Hall was plagued with the problem of a few barefooted students who played bongo drums through the night, and exploded firecrackers on occasion. These students were major exceptions, however; the real onset of the "great unwashed" was yet to come.

One of the immediate changes to occur in respect to dormitory housing was that having to do with racial integration. Previously, much to the disgust of some faculty members, it was almost impossible for a Negro student to obtain dormitory housing. Some Negroes, principally athletes, were given housing in an army barracks near Lake Ruth, but one of Knoblauch's first acts was to tear these down. A "no discrimination" policy was adopted around 1960, and Negroes were freely admitted to various dormitories about the campus.

One of the important facets of the Knoblauch period, notwithstanding the occasional "beatnik," was the important emphasis placed upon neatness and good grooming among the students. Anklets, fashionable with women students for a decade, were replaced with nylon hosiery. In the early 1960's it was important for coeds to own a trench coat, that being in style at the time. The dreaded Macomb winters made parkas fashionable and necessary in the same decade. Bermuda shorts were in during the early 1960's, but rules were established which forbad the wearing of such apparel to class. And too, as everywhere in America, the hemline of dresses continued to rise to the level of the "miniskirt."

As the years of the 1960's rolled by, the habits and customs of students underwent subtle variations. More and more students began to enroll in the institution from the suburban areas about Chicago, and these students, slightly more sophisticated than those from smaller towns in the Military Tract, shifted the ordinary habits of Western's student body. The cost of dating went up—in some cases to twenty dollars—and new and better restaurants began to appear in Macomb. A new kind of morality began to take root. The affluent society had made students more mobile, and thus freer from customary restraints. Student loyalties were slowly transferred from fraternities and sororities to dormitories and, in some cases, to floors in dormitories.

All of these changes were possibly signs of student restiveness yet to come. Fort Lauderdale in Florida became the new Mecca for the vacationing student with a little money and a lot of nerve. Drinking became more than a minor problem for school authorities and there were times when Lake Argyle, a popular rendezvous for the "lakers" (argot for drinking parties), was closed to Western's students after a certain hour.

The new freedom extended further and further into the realms of hitherto closed or inhibited areas of behavior. In 1964 a survey disclosed that one-third of students interviewed admitted to having been slapped, or of slapping in dating situations. Revealing too was the information, released from the same survey, that ten out of seventy-five Western women interviewed admitted to "skinny-dipping" at various times in their lives.

The new freedom inevitably came head-to-head with the old morality. The Chicago, Burlington, and Quincy Railroad had increasing problems in handling students en route to Macomb; in fact, in 1964, there was a rather embarrassing display of disorderliness on board one of the trains carrying students to the city. And further proof of the problem was shown in a single police statistic in 1965. Of all the arrests made in Macomb during the Fall Quarter, thirty-eight percent of these were of college students.

It is common practice to blame today's restiveness among college students upon the Viet Nam War, but how would one explain the actions of such students in the early 1960's? The war had hardly touched upon them; in fact, in previous times of stress, the Cuban missile crisis for example, the Western student body overwhelmingly supported President Kennedy's firm stand against rocket emplacement on that island.

It would appear that the major cause of student unrest, in the early 1960's at least, would have to be tied to the growing size of Western's campus. "Alienation" was a commonly used word and, in retrospect, it seems to have had some validity. No longer were the students close to their instructors. Some classes ballooned to several hundred students in size and, while administrative officials claimed that such classes were just as efficacious as smaller ones, the personal relationship of student and professor was necessarily absent. For this neither the student nor the instructor could be blamed. It was, as some of the students were inclined to say, part of the system.

The new generation of the 1960's, dormitory-housed with several hundred other students and taught in large lecture sections, tended to resist many of the older traditions. The homecoming parade, long one of the spectacles of the school year, began to lose its attractiveness. There was still the usual homecoming decoration of the houses, but something seemed to be missing.

A new language was emerging. A student "aced" a test, a campus policeman was a "boy scout," a "bomb" was a fast car, to "chug" was to drink, a "fink" was a worthless person, an "animal" was a football player or someone connected with sports, to "hack" something was to achieve, and a "hairy" situation was one which involved difficulties.

Yet, by the end of the Knoblauch era, it could be said that the Western student body was well managed, if not industrious. A good reputation had been established by the University's graduates, and the school was looked to as one having a comparatively stable student body. When, in 1969, there was a "sit-in" by students over some minor issue, the general reaction of the surrounding area was one of surprise. Western students, it was said in much of the old Military Tract, were too sensible to indulge in such activities. The incident, as little as it turned out to be, was really part of the times, however. Western, as one might expect, was merely being fashionable. In some way, Harvard, Columbia, and the rest were to be shown that Western Illinois University did exist.

Chapter VI: *The Students*

1. Information from pamphlet published in 1902 and presently in possession of Miss Margaret Wardell.

2. Henninger to Earnest, Nov. 24, 1902; Mrs. Mustain to Henninger, n.d., 1903: *Presidential Collection.*

3. *Sequel,* 1905.

4. *Courier,* May 17, 1918; Feb. 3, 1916.

5. Another rule: any girl caught smoking in Monroe Hall had to apologize to all girls at breakfast.

6. Mr. Harry Anderson to Miss Susan Davies, n.d., 1961; in my possession. See *Sequel,* 1910.

7. *Sequel,* 1905.

8. *The Military Tract: Normal School Quarterly,* June, 1914.

9. Mrs. Martha Davis to Miss Susan Davies, 1961; in my possession.

10. Miss Wilhelmina Bauch to Miss Susan Davies, Mar. 3, 1961; in my possession.

11. Letter from Mrs. Goldia Howes, April 6, 1961.

12. *Ibid.*

13. *Courier,* Dec. 4, 1925.

14. *Ibid.,* Oct. 8, 1936.

15. *Ibid.,* April 26, 1950. The magazine was *Coronet.*

16. *Ibid.,* Oct. 6, 1954.

17. *Ibid.,* Feb. 21, 1940.

18. *Ibid.*, Mar. 19, 1932.

19. *Normal School Quarterly,* June, 1914.

20. *Faculty Minutes,* 1904.

21. *Courier,* April 20, 1917; Nov. 15, 1921.

22. The "forest of Arden" was listed in W.P.A. tour guides as one of the sights of Macomb.

23. Caroline Grote, "The Normal Schools of Illinois," *School News,* July, 1911, p. 515.

24. *Courier,* Jan. 14, 1927.

25. *Ibid.*, Mar. 7, 1935.

26. Advice distributed by Dean of Student Services several years ago, and part of publication entitled "Sixty Easy Ways to Improve Your Personality."

27. *Courier,* May 19, 1948.

28. *Ibid.*, Sept. 6, 1950.

29. *Ibid.*, Dec. 17, 1947; Dec. 12, 1945.

30. *Report of President Beu,* 1949-1950.

31. *Courier,* Nov. 22, 1929.

32. *Ibid.*, May 22, 1940.

33. *Ibid.*, Nov. 12, 1947; Sept. 21, 1949. The ravine was sometimes called the "passion pit."

34. Schlesinger, *op. cit.*, pp. 209-210.

35. *Clionian,* Feb. 1905.

36. *Courier,* Jan. 31, 1919.

37. *Sequel,* 1908.

38. *Ibid.*, 1924, 1928.

39. *Courier,* June 8, 1921. An Oxford University team debated with Western in 1936.

40. *Board Proceedings,* 1917 to 1921. *Sequel,* 1926. One of favorite student haunts was Zahren's Roof Garden.

41. *Sequel,* 1913, 1941, 1928, 1953, 1956, 1944.

CHAPTER VII

The Faculty

The most striking impression which one receives of the faculty of Western Illinois University is that of conservatism and stability. To some extent this is because the earlier presidents intended for it to be so, and employed people of this nature; and to some extent it is because of the nature of the territory in which the school is set. Macomb is essentially a stable town. It has always been so, and may always be so, and for this reason there would be a tendency for the town to draw faculty people of a like nature. Beyond this, there was also the natural development of newer faculty employees to draw themselves into the fabric of the community, and to assume in time the coloration surrounding them.

This is not to say that, throughout the years, the faculty did not have on it strong-minded men and women, or individuals who were inclined to strain the bonds of conformity. It is true, for example, that the man who rides a bicycle through the city streets to his work is probably a member of the Western staff, or that a sizable proportion of the sports cars in town are owned by the faculty and graduate students. But the fact of the matter is that the majority of the staff do not do such things, and that very likely the nature of these people is of a more conservative character than that found on campuses elsewhere.

Through the years, however, there were those whose customs sometimes shocked the town, or the students who came to it. There were others, as the tradition implies, who were absent-minded or whose mental abstractions cut social amenities to shreds.

One faculty member, whose stay on the campus was brief but colorful, could never beat the clock to his early morning classes, and his dress was sometimes a combination of business suit and pajamas. Another, inclined towards forgetfulness, frequently came to class with a large but noticeable ring of toothpaste remnant about his mouth. A third, a social science instructor famous for his inability to remember to do his paper work, could never keep up with changing class rolls and enrolling students. On one occasion his students entered the name of a leading baseball player of the 1930's on his roll and the results were spectacular. Each day this kindly man called his roll, which included the name of the leading hitter in the American League. Legend has it that the same instructor gave a grade to another fictitious character placed on his rolls in a like manner.

Yet, it must be remembered that the "character" as such is to be found no more in the teaching profession than in others; it is just that he is noticed more. Scratch the memories of a Western graduate of any particular period, for instance, and he will come up with some marvelous stories about the medical doctor or of secretaries and caretakers employed by the school during his time as a student.

In a way the more genuinely colorful faculty members of the last seventy years were those of the 1930's. By this time the Morgan administration had endured so long, with all of the staff people hired by this President, that its roots were long indeed. No small wind would blow the structure over, and consequently many of the stronger personalities of the campus were lovably and appealingly interesting. This was particularly true with respect to their driving habits. There was the man, for example, who understood that only half of the road belonged to him, and took it—right in the middle of the highway. All of those who drove towards him had to understand who he was, what position he held, and move out of his way.

There was another fine gentleman who never really became acquainted with all of the gears in his car. He knew what reverse would do, and he usually backed up until he hit something. Beyond this the only other gear he knew was high. Another strong personality could never grasp the reason for stop signs. On one occasion he purchased a new auto which had on the horn button the insignia of the firm which manufactured the vehicle. Shortly thereafter he roared through a stop sign, hit another car, and was imprinted for several weeks with a brand from that insignia.[1]

II.

In the very early days of the institution the morals and manners of Macomb provided strict boundaries within which the faculty had to live. There were almost no autos in town; in fact, Frederick Fairbank, the school's first language instructor, remembered Macomb some sixty years later as a "real horse and buggy" town. "As I recall," wrote Fairbank, "there was only one automobile in Macomb, belonging to the head of one of the potteries." For the faculty member who wished to have some excitement, the railroad provided the only exit to big city life. If one did not indulge in such excursions, he had to find his recreation within the city as well as its strict proprieties. As Fairbank described it:

> For recreation we took long walks or played tennis or hired a horse and buggy from a livery stable and drove around the countryside. One of the pleasantest walks was to go north from the main building to the river and walk east along the south bank to the main north-south highway leading into Macomb. Timber was plentiful then.[2]

Despite the conservatism of the town there were those

faculty members who were willing to defy conventions and live life to the fullest. Oliver M. Dickerson remembered that the younger male members of the faculty in the 1908 era played poker with local businessmen. One teacher, an agriculture instructor, was a daring card player and could be seen quite often about a downtown table; his shirtsleeves rolled up and a cigar in his mouth.

Others who liked exercise of a more physical nature took it without too much town censorship. Many of the faculty before 1910 dined at a "Mrs. Smith's" on Sherman Avenue, and almost always played volley ball in the back yard of this house until mealtime.

The most appealing game was golf, however. During the Bayliss period a golf course was constructed about the front of what is now Sherman Hall, with greens running about to the back of the building. Professor Hursh was very active at this sport, and would sometimes instruct his students on how to play the game. Hursh liked the course so much that there were times when he held his English classes on one of the greens. One student remembers: "In the summertime I would mow the greens at four A.M. so that the faculty golfers could report a good score to their eight o'clock class."³

Beyond these physical activities of the Henninger-Bayliss periods there were the inescapable social interchanges—the teas, the faculty meetings, or the discussion groups. Miss Corbin and Miss Olsen brought the afternoon tea into the early traditions of the school, and it continued all the way to the Beu administration. These were elaborate affairs which were held in social rooms of Sherman Hall, and the *Courier* usually made note of their formality. "The color scheme was green and yellow," said the newspaper about one such affair, "and the flower decorations were roses and pussywillows."

On occasion, faculty members made a special attempt to be "at home" to students. Such receptions were not really held in the homes of the instructors, but were carried out in specific rooms of Sherman Hall. One might suspect that such an activity was considered to be a part of the broad social responsibilities of each faculty member.[4]

Once a year during the first two administrations, each faculty member played host at a formal dinner. Most if not all of the faculty were expected to attend these functions, and most of the faculty enjoyed them. Professor Bonser liked these gatherings and made them into elaborate parties. Professor Drake of the Physics Department also gave elaborate dinners, and generally led the guests in parlor games after the meal.[5]

The faculty teas occasionally evolved into philosophical or political discussions which, in themselves, became traditional. In 1904, for example, the faculty became involved in a lecture-tea program which stretched through the entire year. Miss Hamilton spoke on "Deweyism," Mr. Drake on "Professional Growth," and Mr. Fairbank on "The Roman's Contribution to Civilization." Time came when these meetings developed a tedium which few faculty members wanted to prolong. "After a long and tedious discussion," wrote Professor Burns about one of these teas, "it was resolved to devote twenty minutes to chorus singing in the assembly. . . ."[6]

There was little change in the order of things during the Morgan period. The annual Christmas parties were firm in the tradition, and the compact little faculty met to exchange the usual ties and perfumes. For some few they were moments to be cherished like an old rose. "I want to give joy to my friends and loved ones," exclaimed Miss Grote, "and to help so far as in me lies to carry the message of good tidings to all people."

Besides the annual bridge party at Christmastide, there were all of the social activities which President Morgan so dearly loved. The faculty dinners, Easter egg frolics, and song festivals were command appearances for most of the faculty. Rarely could a more robust male member of the teaching staff evade

these events; that is, short of pleading death or pestilence.
There was a Faculty Club through the 1920's but the President made this into a book review and philosophical society,
which shook instructors coming from lesser intellectual fields.
There was Dr. Garwood's "forest of Arden" again, a Shakespearian setting located to the rear of his house. But Garwood was
almost as strict about attendance as Morgan. Like the President,
Garwood always checked the excuses of absentees.[7]

The most unusual activity of the faculty during the Morgan period was a men's club called "Knights of the Moon."
This groups met in "stag" gatherings in such out-of-the-way
places as on the banks of the Mississippi, or in secluded picnic
areas. In not quite so sedate a setting as the afternoon tea, the
members of the group engaged in a good deal of bantering, some
prankishness, and in occasional gossip. At one such gathering
an instructor, attempting to show his diving form, shot off a
bank in a rare display of speed, only to end up in water only a
foot deep.[8]

The feminine equivalent of the "Knights of the Moon"
was the "Maids of the Mist." Unmarried women, mainly, these
faculty members were still active as an association or club
until about eighteen years ago.

Of the two clubs, the "Knights of the Moon" was the most
interesting. Driving to their activities involved almost as much
daring as being a part of them. Not every "Knight" owned an
automobile and it was necessary for some to ride with the
daredevils who did. The story is told about a famous ride which
Harvey Seal took in a Model T Ford owned and driven by Dean
Fred Currens. Currens was no Barney Oldfield, but on the way
to the Mississippi he kept the car pretty much on two wheels.
Seal, meanwhile, sat in the back, his arms spread-eagled against
the insides of the car. When the Ford finally lurched to a halt,
the passenger emerged, shaking and ashen, and swearing never
to trust himself again in the hands of a dean. He was taken back

to Macomb in another car.[9]

During the Beu period the traditional and formal exercises passed into limbo, for the most part. There were some bridge exchanges, or teas, but they were never compulsory and only those who liked such affairs went to them. There were other more informal affairs at which the staff made a point of showing. The "freshmen picnic" usually brought male members of the faculty out. There were faculty golf contests; particularly an annual one with Illinois State Normal. And, of course, there were varsity football and basketball games which many of the faculty felt it necessary to attend.

III.

On the campus itself, faculty interchange came to evolve around two specific locales. These were the faculty post office, located on the second floor of Sherman Hall, and the "student lounge," located in a ramshackle barracks near the powerhouse. Both became centers for gossip and news, and for discussion and possible intrigue. Though the faculty had no real allotted space in the so-called lounge, there was a booth located to the rear of the building and in the kitchen. The *Courier* described it thusly: "In the rear of the lounge is the kitchen which also has a booth where you can find the members of the faculty discussing the students while in the front part the students discuss the faculty."[10]

Today, the faculty has grown so large that individual communions develop. Those teachers who work in Morgan Hall meet about the coffee cup in a lounge designed for the purpose. Teaching staff which are located near the University Union cross Murray Street to meet in that building. The departments located in Tillman Hall (the old Science Building) have a secluded coffee room on the top floor.

When faculty members meet informally, the chances are that the talk will evolve around classwork, standards, or salary.

The latter has always been a problem with instructors, and since they are human it will always be so. As stated previously, the salaries of earlier days were determined by the president, and what the instructor allowed himself to be employed at in the beginning. Years later Oliver Dickerson, who taught in the 1909 period, complained that he received only $1800 for his first year's work, and received no pay for incidentals. What were the incidentals? As Dickerson put it, he did everything but "mow the lawn."[11]

During Morgan's era the salaries tended to fall off, and the onset of World War I caused so much inflation as to make genuine hardship for those on fixed salaries. As in World War II, faculty members all over the state began to "moonlight" on jobs in 1917 and 1918; that is, until the crisis passed. But the crisis was a real one, and many presidents found it difficult to hold their staffs together while the war "to preserve democracy" was under way. President Shryock, the grand old man of Southern Illinois Normal University, pleaded with the Board: "The younger ones are resigning. . . . I endeavor to assure them that better salaries will be provided in the next budget, but this promise falls upon hesitating ears. The older ones are caught like rats in a trap."

President Brown of Northern Illinois Normal argued: "It is embarrassing to be unable to change salaries any time within a period of twenty-four months, even if some of the members of the faculty are paid less than the men who haul coal and ashes."[12]

The *Courier* of the World War I period got into the act. It editorialized that those "Germans and Poles" near Chicago, the electricians who fixed the clocks in the college, the passenger conductors for the C. B. and Q. Railroad, and assorted technicians about Macomb all earned more money than the faculty. No wonder, the paper concluded, the normal schools of the state had lost 140 teachers in four years.

Eventually the faculties themselves reacted. Western, for instance, sent a delegation to Springfield composed of Currens, Simpkins, and others for the purpose of pleading for salary increases.[13]

Just how low were salaries in the period surrounding World War I? In analyzing such facts and figures, one must remember that President Morgan was a conservative man in salary administration. He generally made his Board requests lower than those of other normal school presidents, he tended to keep his faculty concentrated in the lower ranks, and he prided himself upon turning unused appropriations back to the state. In 1918 most of the faculty salaries were in the $1000 to $2000 bracket. Morgan's report to the Board in the following year showed that the school had fewer professors than all of the state normal schools but one, and that this rank at Western drew a lower income than comparable levels elsewhere. The average pay for full professors in Macomb was $2595.

Two other schools in the teachers college system had more assistant professors than Western (there was no associate level here) , but the average salary in this rank was lower in Macomb than elsewhere, being $1877. Only on the instructors' level did Western lead the rest, having more people serving at this rank, and having the highest salary average which was $1589.[14]

It might be surprising for today's teaching staff to know that, in Morgan's era, few instructors actually knew which rank they held. In fact, many did not even know that there was a professorial ranking in the school. Only the President and the Dean knew the ranks and salaries of all, and it was the President who determined both. In theory Morgan used student evaluations and those of the Dean to pass out pay increases. In reality, however, one might suspect that Mr. Morgan's evaluation was the only one which really counted. Still, student evaluations tended to have an adverse effect upon faculty morale. As one instructor of the time put it: "My great aim during this phase of the school's history was to be popular (with the students), and not necessarily good."[15]

By 1922 salaries in the normal schools were brought to a subsistence level. Though Western still lagged behind the other schools, the impulse of the general raises was felt at Macomb as well as at Carbondale or DeKalb. A study of increases in the period tended to show that, all along the line, staff members earned a thousand dollars more during the academic year than previously. This development, plus continued financial considerations by the Board, served to ameliorate the bad conditions which had existed through 1917 and 1918.[16]

Through the Beu administration, salaries continued to lag behind those given at other state teachers colleges, with but the exception of a few years. This persisted, despite attempts by President Beu to get adjustments. Finally, after 1960, in the Knoblauch administration, Western's faculty salaries caught up with and surpassed those at sister institutions.[17]

IV.

While salaries are given a great deal of conversational attention by Western's faculty, a close second might be found in teaching conditions or classroom standards. It might be pertinent in this respect to indicate that Western's faculty has seldom been research motivated in the past. Real scholarly production, research for the purpose of extending the frontier of man's knowledge, has been limited to say the least.

The resignation of Oliver M. Dickerson after Bayliss's death was a turning point with regard to research. From the early Morgan years on the inclination of would-be scholars was to leave Macomb, and the teaching instructor became the desired role. It is true that certain instructors did contribute by way of textbooks; Dr. Glenn Ayre and Dr. Clyde Beighey, as examples. But in truth, it would take a good deal of searching to find any important original contributions to research during the seventy years of the existence of Western's faculty. Dickerson, of course, produced an important book when he was here, and there are a few other scattered cases, but research for the sake of research is not in the Western pattern.

This is not to say that there is a stigma to be attached to instructional aspects of campus life. Western's faculty has always regarded this to be of paramount importance, and it has geared its efforts to that end. One is reminded here of one instructor who was scheduled for ten credit hours of instruction during each day; an occasion which happened not too long ago. Doing research while carrying that kind of a teaching load is an impossibility.

This is not to say that the faculty at Western has ignored scholarly effort altogether. Many noble individuals have sincerely tried to keep abreast of their fields, and others have worked hard to produce articles, book reviews, and textbooks in their areas of study. But, for many of Western's instructors, the sixteen hour weekly teaching load, plus the surfeit of committee assignments, served to sap their energies until the beginning of the Knoblauch administration. Only then was the load reduced, and some kind of premium placed upon writing as well as research.

V.

The traditional burden at Western has been in teaching. Through the years, the student body, which is on the receiving end of this effort, has presented a variety of types, with most of the young men and women coming from small towns in the Military Tract. In the very early days many of the students were from the farming areas; earnest young people who had made their way through country schools to the normal school level. The transition to life in Macomb was difficult, not only from a social standpoint but also in terms of scholastic achievement. This was how the faculty had to look upon their pupils, and much sympathy and understanding were needed in order to bring student achievement up to acceptable levels.[18]

In the early years it also meant forcing the student to catch up with more sophisticated scholars elsewhere by the dint of hard work. As the *Courier* proclaimed in 1905: "Each professor thinks his class has twenty-four hours each day in which to prepare his special subject, while in fact the Sophomores recite every hour in the day but one, and must prepare their lessons by the aid of midnight oil."[19]

It was the same lack of polish in the early student which led to compulsory attendance at chapel or assembly. Here, argued the faculty, some kind of magic might occur which would lift the student from the influence of village mediocrity to the cultural level of the entertainment provided in these gatherings. There was no way for the wayward student to escape. Everyone had to go, faculty and students alike, and the attendance was carefully checked in each instance. Each person had to fill out a slip indicating his presence, and each slip was tabulated by the registrar.

Programs included a variety of topics and numbers. One day there might be an illustrated lecture given with the aid of an "illuminated lantern." Another program might consist of a type of community sing, or readings by members of the English Department. Occasionally there was imported talent—a visiting lecturer or a returning alumnus to tell of his experiences in the wide world of teaching.[20]

With the improvements of the English, drama, and music departments over the years, the chapel programs tended to diminish in importance. A study of the kind of subject matter handled in classes during the 1920's, for example, indicates that the individual student was effectively receiving in regular class sessions the kind of information which was formerly forced upon him during the chapel periods. In 1924, for instance, one could find a modern drama class making a special study of

Ibsen's plays, particularly "Ghosts," currently on tour with Eleanora Duse in the starring role.

In English classes in the same week, students were discussing in open forum the Bok Peace Plan, as well as other methods by which war could be avoided. Professor Schuppert's history classes were engaged in a hand-to-hand struggle with written biographies of such famous Americans as Washington and Lincoln; and the art classes were designing posters which illustrated good health practices. In the advanced literature classes, students read the works of George Ade, Irvin S. Cobb, and other American humorists. And in physiology, students were making studies (in class) of the effects of drugs and alcohol upon the human body.[21]

These excursions into the world of knowledge do not seem too different from those taken by students today. One might suspect that much of the same material is handled these days, but with mild corrections: i. e., the United Nations supplanting the Bok Peace Plan, Arthur Miller in place of Ibsen, or perhaps Robert Lowell in the place of George Ade. In a sense, the type of instructional materials has changed but little; and, one may add, this may also be true to some degree in the realm of science. It is possibly true, however, that the quality of instruction is superior today over that of yesteryear. This would unquestionably be so if one were to consider the number of doctorates on the staff as being indicative of a standard of instructional excellence.

Nevertheless, with respect to the faculty role in the university structure, little has changed. The individual staff person finds that a good deal of his time is taken with the primary consideration of teaching, and a good deal more of his time is taken with such problems as counseling, committee work, grading papers, composing examinations, and attending faculty or student functions. He still must give a large slice of his emotional and physical self on the altar of the laggard student, much in the same manner as his predecessors. For many of the staff this is well worth the effort. Some students are saved, though it must be added that many more are not. Still, working for the purpose of salvaging one worthy but undeveloped student seems to be deep in the Western tradition.

During President Morgan's time, there was never any great pressure upon the faculty to conform to certain pass or fail percentages, except indirectly. Morgan's wish was to have a staff filled with "understanding" instructors who would not be extreme in any direction. Furthermore, as has been pointed out, students did evaluate instructors, purportedly helping in determining pay increases. This qualification in salary determination served to turn the stoniest professor's heart to jelly.

During the later Morgan years, when the faculty began to change somewhat, the administration felt it necessary to suggest a grading curve to new instructors. This called for a $\%3.59$ fail rate, a $\%3.59$ "A" rate, a $\%23.84$ "B" rate, a $\%23.84$ "D" rate, and the remainder in the "C" category.

This curve was only proposed, however, and one suspects that the actual bulge in the college grading curve was on the high side. Openly Morgan seldom made references to grading practices, except to make occasional announcements during assembly meetings about extremities in the grading situation. These words were usually followed by some sort of inspirational lecture to students and faculty about the necessity of working harder in order to bring grades up.[22]

In the 1950's there were complaints, both vocal and published, that standards had fallen to a disastrous level. Looking back, it seems that though the school should have been better, it was never as bad as the critics claimed. The departments which had always been rigorous in standards were rigorous then, and the departments which were more tolerant in grading then had always been so.

The disparity between departments in terms of grading

exists today, just as it exists at most colleges and universities. Some areas at Western still have difficulty in finding a few poor students throughout an entire year, while others have a high percentage of them.

The real fact of the matter is that the good departments, and the poorer ones, are generally known by the students and by faculty members. The large dormitories, housing many hundreds of students, allow for widely dispersed insights into which teachers are hard and easy, where cheating can be carried out, where the subject matter is shallow, and what teachers in more difficult departments grade the easiest.

A wide range of philosophies and attitudes is therefore present on the Western campus. A school which was once totally teacher-training in its aims is on its way toward becoming a true university. One is reminded here of James Burns' analysis of the Western faculty in 1916, and how it pointed up that over half of the teaching staff was of Presbyterian and Scots-Irish backgrounds. There was a oneness which is not quite so evident in this day of growth and change. A faculty which, at one time, did not have a single Jew or Catholic, now has a sprinkling of creeds and a variation of national backgrounds.[23]

The same is true of training, degrees, and educational approaches, all of which might lead some to complain that things are not just what they used to be, or that there is too much conflict in ideas and philosophies. This, once again, is part of the university concept. Three hundred years ago a university president in Europe complained:

> The entire faculty should be kept in friendship, in contact with one another, and in unity so that youth may see from their example what the University with time, will teach them. . . . The professors should not speak badly to their own students of the teaching and scholarship of their colleagues, but rather encourage one another's scholarship.[24]

Chapter VII: *The Faculty*

1. Some of this information comes from Mr. Kimbrough Shake.
2. Frederick Fairbank to this writer, Feb., 1961.
3. Miss Wilhelmina Bauch, Mr. Harry Anderson, and Mrs. Selena Dunlap wrote letters to me in 1961, and this correspondence from former students is the source of much of this information.
4. *Faculty Minutes*, 1902; *Courier*, April 6, 1916.
5. Communication from Mr. Russell P. Drake, Feb. 6, 1961.
6. *Faculty Minutes*, April, 1902.
7. Miss Grote's revealing comment comes from the *Courier*, Dec. 23, 1909.
8. Mr. Wayne Wetzel, retired, is the source of this information. The "Maids of the Mist" were still in existence in 1949.
9. Mr. Wetzel once again.
10. *Courier*, Sept. 21, 1949. More than once I have heard faculty members indicate regret over the disappearance of the old post office.
11. O. M. Dickerson to this writer, Feb., 1961. Dickerson also said: "Whatever needed to be done was done willingly. The fact that it was outside the teacher's regular field did not matter. Everybody did what came his way. . . . It was our school and we were proud of it."
12. *Board Proceedings*, 1920, pp. 19-29.
13. *Ibid.*, pp. 45-47. *Courier*, April 18, 1921, also.
14. *Board Proceedings*, 1918, pp. 66-67. Also p. 24 of 1919 *Proceedings.*
15. Mr. Walter Eller, retired, is the source of the information concerning the fact that faculty members did not know what rank they held. Naturally I would not disclose the source of the quote.
16. *Board Proceedings*, 1921, p. 25.
17. The chapter dealing with President Beu's problems contains information on salaries of that period. The present position of faculty salaries at Western is good.
18. Communication from Mr. Guy Hoyt, Feb. 15, 1961.
19. *Courier*, Dec. 1905.
20. "Seminar Programs, 1904-1905," a pamphlet published by the school in 1904. Miss Hamilton spoke on John Dewey. Mr. Drake on "Professional Growth," and Mr. Fairbank on "The Roman's Contribution to Civilization." The pamphlet is now in the possession of Miss Margaret Wardell.
21. *Courier*, Jan. 25, 1924.
22. *Faculty Handbook*, 1939-1940; *Courier*, Dec. 7, 1917.
23. *Courier*, Jan. 20, 1916. Mr. Burn's analysis of national background of Western's faculty showed four of Puritan stock, seven of "Virginia Cavalier" ancestry, fourteen of Scots-Irish background, and the remainder from English, German, Swedish, and Huguenot stock.
24. *American Association of University Professors Bulletin*, Winter, 1960.

CHAPTER VIII

The Leatherneck Tradition

In the first ten years of Western's existence there was a serious attempt to establish a sense of tradition within the institution. Unfortunately, much of this effort was rooted in barren soil almost resistant to growth, and the newly born foci of loyalty were swept away with each succeeding president. Morgan turned the school away from the liberal arts concept, for example; and lesser traditions—the old well or the ravine— fell as victims to the decisions of later leaders. One area in which tradition did flourish was that of athletics. This was not only wrapped around individuals associated with Western and intercollegiate sports, but with winning or losing.

The aura about athletics on the Western campus is impossible to define in terms of how, when, why, or where. It is not that Western has totally dominated in the athletic conference with which it has associated itself through the years, for it most certainly has not. It is not really because Western's students are so vitally interested in sport that it precludes anything else, for that is a debatable point. It is not totally because of an avid town interest in the school's sport activities that the teams have done well, for each college has its so-called "subway alumni." So it must be by reason of part of many factors that Western's teams have striven extraordinarily hard, and that a Leatherneck tradition has arisen.

Almost fundamental in the development of the Western

Normal School was the teachers college tradition; that Western should do well what Knox or Monmouth, schools to the north, were not attempting to do. When Morgan became the chief executive of the school, he moved directly into the areas of vocational instruction. Furthermore he would provide teachers for those fields in which there was a short supply of instructors. Physical education, manual training, and other such fields were emphasized.

The liberal arts approach was driven from the school, and the program was supposedly fitted to the needs of the geographic entity of Western Illinois. If one were to study the size of various departments in the college in the 1920's and 1930's, he would find the greatest enrollments in business courses, home economics, physical education, and special education fields. One must suppose that, all in all, the decline of liberal arts and the rise of vocationalism brought the athletically inclined student in the direction of Macomb.

The gradual growth of athletic tradition at Western had a stuttering beginning however. There were teams from the beginning, and one of the first doctrines to which President Henninger committed himself was that of having an athletic program. One month after Sherman Hall was opened, he indicated that he had given sixty dollars to the sports program and that he wished to schedule a series of games. Since normal schools played high schools in those days, he wrote to the principal in nearby Table Grove, Illinois, and asked that a football game be arranged.

Because schools were under few restraints in those days, and because normal schools were often trounced by high school teams which employed "ringers" to play for them, Henninger asked for proof that Table Grove would field a legitimate team. The reply was amusing. "I am willing to vouch for every man on the team," replied the Table Grove principal. "They are every one a gentleman. They are not under pledge (to stop

drinking) this year . . . but what some of them do that what
you might say is bad is smoke."[1]

The game, along with other such contests, was scheduled,
even though Western did not have a coach. Since the whole
athletic program was haphazardly run in those days, Henninger's solution to this was to ask the Knox College coach to
come down for "two days" and to get the team in shape. With
such inadequate coaching and the short shrift given to conditioning, the normal team had a miserable first year.[2]

Basketball as an activity in the college also found rough
going in the beginning. The gymnasium was not finished, and
the boys who wished to practice had to do so on the rare sandlot
courts found about town. Games were scheduled in the same
manner as those in football, with Henninger himself correspon-
ding with principals about the area. Indicative of the situation
in this sport in 1903 is a letter written by Henninger to a principal: "We have heard that your high school would like to play
a game of ball with the State Normal team," he wrote. "We
haven't won a game yet; but perhaps we could arrange to play
you a game."[3]

By 1903 Henninger had organized the first athletic board
of control which consisted of the president, two faculty members, and two students. This committee proceeded to broaden
the whole scope of the sports program to include inter-institu-
tional games in football, men's basketball, and girl's basketball,
the latter being quite as important a phase of athletics in this
period as those participated in by men. Professor Drake, the
physics instructor, managed the girls to a successful season,
but the boys did not do nearly as well in basketball. It may be
well to note, however, that both DeKalb Normal and Augustana
College provided part of the opposition for the season.[4]

In the remaining years of the Henninger administration, the athletic program became firmly rooted in the fabric of
the institution. Football was fitted to an expanded schedule

which included such teams as "Old Normal," DeKalb Normal, Carthage College, and various high schools including that at Lewistown. The basketball schedule was likewise enlarged to include some of the same schools plus Hedding College at Abingdon, Illinois. Drake eventually took over the management of the football squad, though it appears from the records that the actual coaching was done by one of the members of the team. Football games were played at the old "fair grounds" in Macomb, and basketball games were played in the partly finished school gymnasium.[5]

Unfortunately the caliber of play in both basketball and football was seldom up to the level provided by some of the high schools in the area. In those days the Western teams were staffed by both normal and high school students mainly interested in finishing the requirements of the school rather than in winning games. The high schools, however, often enrolled local roughnecks during the fall of the year only to win games. Many of these noble characters were well up in age, and there were many instances in Illinois in which it was possible for students to play as many as ten seasons of football. The remainder of the time they worked in the coal mines, or on the farm.[6]

Equipment for both the Western players and the opposition was nominal. Sometimes a helmet was provided, but most of the players preferred to do without. There were no shoulder pads, little padding of any other kind, and no doctor on hand to give treatment. In most cases teams had just enough players to field a squad, so if one individual was hurt he either continued to play or his team did without the full quota of team members.

Plays were usually run off in a type of "T-formation," with a variation of the old flying wedge as the major maneuver. Though the play was exceedingly rough, with fists and elbows constantly flying, the players were not ordinarily big. The average weight of the Western team in 1904 was only one hundred and fifty-two pounds. Nor did the existence of physical handicap serve to stop a man from playing a game, as Professor Roy Sallee showed. He played for a Western team in this early period despite the handicap of having only one arm.

Though it was likely at this time that girls' basketball drew the most interest from the student body, it is obvious from both *Sequel* and *Courier* files that football gained many adherents to the sport. There is something elemental about the game, something reminiscent of the gladiatorial contests of old—it pits the irresistible against the immovable, and that seems to be the way most people look at it. One cannot help but smile at an early Western editor's description of such a contest, and the hopes for the future.

> The season opened with bright prospects; all the old veterans were in line, each man a character and star in his particular position. Happy Cordell, who no defeat could ever subdue, Sutton to whom the fiercest scrimmage was like "money from home." Rexroat, the handsome center, across whose noble brow there passed a frown. Benjamin, the irresistible. Thompson, whose commanding voice could be heard amid the fiercest din of grinding muscle and cracking heads. The new material seemed promising.[7]

When Bayliss became the President, there was a sudden reaction against the emphasis which Henninger had begun to place upon athletics. This was part of a nationwide concern about the growing commercialism and violence in intercollegiate sports. There were a number of deaths due to football throughout the country, and the President of the United States, Theodore Roosevelt, was on record about the problem of overstressed sports programs.

Many of the Western faculty likewise deplored the direction in which local athletics were headed with the cheering sections, the newly formed pep band, and increasingly bitter relations between this and other institutions. Bayliss's attitude, though at odds with the people of the town, was similar. He felt that Western did not have the funds to put on a "big show" which the public wanted.

When Bayliss asked for faculty support to abolish football he met little opposition; only O. M. Dickerson, the history instructor, pleading the case for the game. Bayliss's decision was to allow the football program to continue, but with only two games on the schedule. Dickerson was appointed to coach the team at no extra pay, and with no assistance. Dickerson was also the team trainer.

The student body raised no great objection to the move. The *Courier* argued that the fun had gone out of athletics so corrupted with professionalism, and that activity in which "fun" resulted deserved most of the college funds designated for sports. There was too much "unhealthy rivalry" in athletics, continued the paper, and there was too much bitterness between competing institutions. The individual athlete had too much strain placed upon him and the betting which attended big games offered too much temptation to the players. Physical training, the *Courier* concluded, was not just for the eleven or nine players involved, but was something which all students were entitled to receive.[8]

President Bayliss eventually relented somewhat in his attitude concerning intercollegiate contests. Football, under Dickerson, gradually enlarged its program to include games with the Blandinsville High School, Gem City Business College (Quincy), the Knox "seconds," and Carthage College. It is interesting that only the second team of Knox played the Western team. The explanation lies in the fact that "Old Siwash" was one of the football powers of the Midwest.

The old evils returned to the game, however: the broken bones, violent crowds swarming upon the field to attack the referee, and the abuses concerning the playing of "non-student' substitutes. One old graduate still remembers the horrible physical beating inflicted on his team by a high school eleven composed of twenty-five year old players.

There was a new football field at Western though; a spot now occupied by Tillman Hall. A rather misshapen wooden grandstand was erected and this edifice stood, termites and all, until almost the half-century mark. Here track meets as well as baseball contests were held. Basketball was played in the Sherman Hall gymnasium, a room now filled in with registration and computing facilities. Drake continued to manage the round-ball sport.[9]

President Morgan brought new changes and emphasis in the total athletic program. His total educational philosophy was vague, but he did have something to say about intercollegiate sports. "I am interested in clean and wholesome athletics," he once commented. "It is this sort of athletics that the members of the faculty and the student body will back up." That Morgan liked sports is shown by the fact that, even after he was appointed President, he played on the faculty baseball team.

One sees the difference between Bayliss and Morgan on the issue of athletics as a definitive one. Bayliss thought of athletics as totally extra-curricular; Morgan considered them to be part of the institutional educational program. "Nothing destroys the good name of a school more quickly than for the public to feel that there is crookedness on the part of an athletic coach," Morgan once said, "or an athletic team either in playing bona fide students of the school. . . or students who are below grade." Honor and honesty and the respect of others were the ingredients of an acceptable athletic program, he argued.[10] Parenthetically, it might be pointed out that, during Morgan's presidency, the football team had to forfeit a number of games in one season because it played a "semi-pro" athlete.

New developments occurred under Morgan which changed

the entire athletic program of the school. Girls' basketball still remained as an attraction and an intercollegiate sport, but the decline in emphasis was real and apparent.[11] The football team limped through the season of 1914 with a makeshift team and very little coaching, for Dickerson had left with the advent of Morgan. Later in the same year the first real "director" of athletics was employed at Western with the appointment of E. S. Dowell. Dowell had received an A.B. from Oberlin College and an M.A. from the University of Illinois, and his teaching specialty was history.

The results of the appointment were fairly immediate. A bigger football schedule was arranged with other colleges, and there was a general upgrading of the whole program. The football team, for the first time, received adequate equipment. Helmets of a sort and slightly padded sweaters were distributed to the players, though many of the students continued to play helmetless and without the primitive extra-shoulder and hip pads issued by the coach.

None of this helped in terms of victory, for Knox slaughtered the team. The remainder of the season was calamitous.[12] The football and basketball teams did win student support, however; an achievement which was not always forthcoming in that day and age. The *Courier* found the new emotionalism at the games to be ridiculous. "There is no limit on your behavior as a spectator," it stated, "you may whisper, talk, sing, whistle, shout, yell, whoop, or do anything to work yourself up into such a frenzy that you feel as if you could go down and eat the visiting team alive. . . ."[13]

The first five years of Morgan's presidency brought more changes in the athletic program. Another "new" coach for football and basketball was employed in 1915. He was Erskine L. Jay, who had attended Platteville Normal in Wisconsin as well as the University of Wisconsin. Jay was not to have great success with his teams at Western, but it should be stated that he was the first coach employed at the school who had a central interest in sports. He did not have peripheral fields and he was, according to those who knew him, a "tough" and competitive man.

Jay continued to build up the athletic program and scheduled such schools as Shurtleff College, McKendree, Southern Illinois Normal, and Illinois College at Jacksonville. In addition, Jay developed a stronger approach to Western Academy athletics. This school, he felt, should serve as a feeder for college teams. Mr. E. A. Franquemont was employed by President Morgan to coach an Academy team, and for several seasons he had some success in that respect.[14]

In 1919 the college joined the Illinois Intercollegiate Athletic Conference. This assemblage of schools, called by many the "little nineteen," provided some of the strongest intercollegiate competition in the Midwest. In time, the state colleges came to dominate it, and many of the private schools began to withdraw. In 1937 ten of the members withdrew, and in 1942 the conference collapsed when six more schools bowed out of competition.

The I.I.A.C. was fundamentally helpful to Western's emerging athletic program, however. Basketball and football schedules were further strengthened, and no more high schools were listed as opponents.[15] In several cases intense rivalries resulted. This was especially true in the case of Carthage College; an athletic association which caused the administrations of both schools some embarrassment. Pranks, sometimes harmful, were played by both schools, and there was some property damage which resulted from them.[16]

With the development of such emotionalism there were certain inevitable and concomitant results. The first "pep" student organization emerged during the 1920's and was called the "Howling Teachers" or the "Screaming Widows." Thus began the cycle of athletic escalation: the public demanding winning teams; and the winning teams bringing about more public interest.[17]

The increasing fan interest in the results of the games had its impact upon the Western coaching staff. During the 1920's there was a rapid succession of athletic directors, as incumbents left for one reason or another. Jay retired to a farm in Wisconsin, and his place was taken by Mr. C. J. Roberts, who coached basketball, and Mr. W. A. Cleveland, who coached football. Both men had bad seasons; in fact, it was hard to find a victory registered in either sport. Mr. R. E. Haberman succeeded them both in 1921 and though he seemed quite competent (Knox called him in 1922), the teams had only average successes.

In 1922, Howard Hawkes was employed as the athletic director and he endured the problems of providing a winner much longer than his predecessors. The pressures common to modern coaching were common then, and more than once a college would be shaken by incidents arising from them. On one occasion at Western, for example, it was rumored that a coach was taken out to the countryside by local roughnecks and forced to walk home. Then, as stated before, Western was required to forfeit some hard earned victories because it had played a "semi-pro" quarterback on its team.[18]

Hawkes' years as athletic director did bring a turning point in Western's sports program. There were more victories than defeats, and more talented players began to appear on the campus. The basketball team of 1923-1924 was a good example of the change with such fine performers as Ralph Barclay, Morris Hesh, and Harry Newburn. Hawkes was able to turn over to his successor in 1926, Ray Hanson, one of the finest teams ever to wear the Western uniform. It included Hesh, Leroy Morley, and the first of a long line of fine Negro athletes to attend the college, Ernest Page.[19]

The arrival of Hanson in 1926 was marked by no fanfare. No one could have known or guessed the extent of the man's future contributions to the athletic traditions of the institution, or that in time the students of other generations would assume that Hanson "was here first and Western State was built around him."[20]

He is a most colorful man, even today. As the athletic director he gave the impression of complete disorganization; a guise which led many to misinterpret his abilities. In reality, Hanson has a quick and alert mind which is full of little surprises and traps. He has no small amount of physical and mental courage, as is attested to by his service to the Marine Corps in both world wars. During the first of those conflicts he took part in engagements at Belleau Wood, Soissons, Pont a Moussin, Champagne, and St. Mihiel, and came out of the fighting with the Distinguished Service Cross.

After his release from the Corps he did graduate work at Springfield Teachers College in Massachusetts, and later studied coaching under such significant masters as Knute Rockne (thus Hanson's nickname of "Rock").[21]

His arrival on the Western campus was the signal of a new era, for through no encouragement from him a "cult of personality" grew up around the man. His tendency to faint at crucial points of a game, his large automobiles, his erratic driving, and his manner of expression helped him to become an extremely popular man. Hanson, and all that came with him, seemed to be so appropriate for the new gymnasium which was opened in 1928 (now Brophy Hall).

It was not long before Western, together with Hanson, achieved some kind of national publicity. The new athletic director obtained permission from the Marine Corps to adopt the word "leatherneck" as a team symbol for the college, and the institution became the only one in the country entitled to use the name. At approximately the same time Hanson, with the support of President Morgan, embarked upon a kind of cleanup crusade against the use of profanity by team players.

Despite an occasional suspension of a performer, the "basic English" as used by the players remained unchanged, and probably the only thing gained was a good deal of national publicity on the subject. Hanson did achieve significant changes in various game rules, however. It was this man as much as anyone else who probably changed the game of basketball from one of tactics to one of speed. In 1932, for instance, Hanson's proposal to install the so-called "center line" in basketball was the first of many steps in this direction.[22]

It must be written, and Hanson would probably agree, that Western's fortunes were never consistently good under his command. He had his good teams in both major sports, and he had his bad ones. His basketball team finished second in the conference in 1928, but his football teams in the same period were not exceptional. His basketball teams of 1932-1933 were brilliant and starred such individuals as Gib Love and the two Grigsby boys, but once again football fortunes left much to be desired.

In the mid-1930's, however, Hanson hit a level of performance which would be hard to emulate. The excellent basketball team composed of Woods, Laeding, Means, and others won a share of the conference title in 1935. In 1938 the first undisputed conference championship in basketball was won by a team consisting of such men as Hughes, Willard, and Stewart.

The latter was the same Paul Stewart who led the football team to the conference championship in 1939; a brilliant performer rated by many as unequalled in the history of the school.* It may be added that Hanson's tendency was to present schedules in every sport which caught the interest both of students and townspeople; and the basketball schedule of 1939-1940, for example, included such prominent schools as Oregon, St. Louis University, and Purdue.[23]

The coming of the war served to bring a temporary end to these phenomenal sports successes. Hanson left to rejoin the

*I saw Stewart play, and he was indeed exceptional.

Marine Corps, and his successors, among them "Wix" Garner, tried valiantly to keep the athletic program going despite the scarcity of manpower. It was a common comment during these hard years that both the football and basketball teams were composed of just anybody who cut his hair close. During the 1943 football season the school barely fielded a team, and the beatings inflicted upon it were memorable. The basketball team of 1944 was composed of but thirteen players and their successes, like those in football, were limited to the area of character building.[24]

As soon as the war ended, President Beu, along with Hanson, worked diligently to bring Western to winning ways in all phases of athletics. Garner, likely at his own wish, returned to his first love, the coaching of baseball; and Harold Ave, a former coach at Eastern Illinois State College, was given the football reins. Leroy Morley took over the leadership of the basketball team, and Western was on its way to those amazing sports successes which marked its post-World War II period.

Ave's record in football was quite adequate, but in 1949 he gave way to Vincent DiFrancesco who, during his stay in Macomb, compiled a rather enviable record in the sport. It was so outstanding, in fact, that DiFrancesco left for what he thought were greener fields, a head coaching position at Iowa State University, leaving a vacancy to be filled by the employment of Wesley Stevens. Stevens served a few years, moving to an administrative position in the university, and Lou Saban, a former professional player in the National Football League, took his place. When Saban left in the late 1950's in order to return to professional football, the head coaching position in the university was filled by Arthur Dufelmeier, an assistant to the previous three coaches.[25] Dufelmeier is a likeable and competent coach whose record of victories was very adequate until recent years. The recruiting and keeping of capable players seemed to become more difficult in the last three seasons, however. Mr.

Dufelmeier resigned in 1969, and was replaced by Dr. Dale Mudra, whose coaching experience has been in the southwestern United States.

Mr. Leroy Morley, in basketball, survived a few tough years following the end of World War II, always fielding well coached teams but having no conference winners. In 1949 he brought together his first good team, and from that time to only recently he enjoyed one good season after another. His most excellent teams were in the mid-1950's, particularly one quintet made up of Stoner, Rios, the Talbot brothers, and Charles Schramm. Several of these men had been in larger universities but had made their way to Western to form perhaps the most brilliant of Morley's teams.[26]

It is difficult to put into words the philosophy which prevails at Western concerning the place of athletics in the University. In the past there were many faculty members who felt that more significance was placed upon the total program than it really deserved. There were some who felt that the state and local reputation of the school was not helped by what appeared to them to be overemphasis on both football and basketball.

Still, the faculty in general supported the teams with enthusiasm. Victories are not always won by talent alone, imported or otherwise, but are the results of the will to win. And Western, in most cases, has had that.

Now Ray Hanson is retired. Dufelmeier and Morley have stepped down from their coaching positions; Mr. Guy Ricci having taken the basketball coaching job. "Wix" Garner and Harold Ave are also retired; both men now making a valiant attempt to wear out the Macomb Country Club golf course. So it goes! Men leave but a tradition lingers.

Chapter VIII: *The Leatherneck Tradition*

1. Henninger to A. C. Norton, Nov. 8, 1902, *President's Collection*. Henninger wrote that the average weight of Western's team was one hundred and fifty pounds, and that the average age was twenty. Also G. W. Ross to Henninger, Nov. 11, 1902, *Ibid.*

2. Henninger to John McLean, Nov. 21, 1902, *ibid.*

3. Henninger to principal, Abingdon High School, May 19, 1903; Henninger to George Arnold, Mar. 16, 1903, *ibid.*

4. *Sequel*, 1904. Dekalb was defeated; Augustana won.

5. *Sequel*, 1905. The 1904 football season showed a five won, two lost record, with average weight of the team being one hundred and fifty-two pounds.

6. Mr. Wayne Wetzel helped me with this.

7. *Clionian*, Feb., 1905.

8. *Courier*, Dec. 9, 1909. Also *Courier*, Jan 1907. In a communication written to me in Feb., 1961, O. M. Dickerson states that there was a national movement to reform college athletics at this time. He writes that President Bayliss presented the idea of dropping football to a faculty meeting, but when Dickerson objected the President "considered for a minute and said that he had no coach . . . would I take charge of football . . . no extra pay." Dickerson states that he would go to the practice field at four o'clock in the afternoon, practice until five, and then give each man a rubdown.

9. *Sequel*, 1909, 1911. Wayne Wetzel recalls these games with glee; particularly how the referee, upon occasion, was forced to get out of town as fast as possible.

10. *Courier*, Feb. 17, 1921; Oct. 8, 1920.

11. Mrs. Earl Jackson to Miss Susan Davies, April 12, 1961; in my possession. Mrs. Jackson remembers with pride how she scored winning basket against Hedding College, and how after each game a lunch was prepared by the host team.

12. *Sequel*, 1915. The schedule included Knox, Monmouth College, Christian University, and several high schools.

13. *Courier*, Jan. 27, 1916. The paper states: "The coach tosses the ball into the air and extemporizes on the first variation of 'The Mocking Bird.' Two players simultaneously soar toward the zenith and try to poke their fingers into each other's eyes."

14. *Sequel*, 1916. Also, Mr. Ray Hanson's recollection concerning Jay.

15. *Homecoming Bulletin*, Western Illinois State College, 1949.

16. Many faculty members still in service of school can remember the athletic rivalry between Western and Carthage.

17. *Sequel*, 1923.

18. *Sequel*, 1921, 1922; *Courier*, Oct. 8, 1920. Also, the recollections of Professor Walter Eller, the band director during the 1920's.

19. *Sequel*, 1926.

20. *Courier*, Nov. 12, 1947.

21. *Ibid.*, Oct. 22, 1926.

22. *Ibid.*, Nov. 12, 1926; April 7, 1932. When Hanson arrived at Western, some of the players still played without helmets.

23. *Sequel*, 1931, 1935, 1936, 1938, 1940.

24. *Ibid.*, 1944. The football team lost every game but one; the basketball team had a four won and eleven lost record.

25. The new football field was begun in 1947. The football team of 1949 lost only one game; that to Wayne State University. It also won the third annual Corn Bowl game. The basketball record for 1950 was seventeen and six.

26. The basketball team of 1956 is listed as having only three losses.

CHAPTER IX

President Beu and the Beginnings of Expansion

On October 16, 1942, the faculty of Western Illinois State Teachers College convened for the purpose of inaugurating a new president of the institution. His name was Dr. Frank Andrew Beu.

According to information published in a local Macomb newspaper, Dr. Beu was a man of some six feet in height, carrying a well distributed one hundred and eighty pounds. He had had an interesting career in American education, having taken a baccalaureate at Northwestern with a major in social science and English, followed by an M.A. at the same institution. The latter degree, according to news reports, was granted upon the basis of a thesis entitled "The Intelligence of Athletes and Non-Athletes."

Later he completed the Ph.D. in Education at the University of Chicago with a dissertation upon the legal basis of the organization and administration of state normal schools in the Midwest.

In the time between the baccalaureate and the doctorate he taught and coached at Hebron, Illinois, and eventually acted as superintendent in the same place. Later he took a position as professor of methodology at Eastern Illinois State Teachers College, and in time became the Dean of Instruction in the same institution. His list of publications seemed impressive to the Board and included a textbook on American education written in collaboration with a colleague at Eastern.[1]

The impact of Beu's personality upon Western was to be profound, and it brought about broad changes in the school. Morgan had guided a taut ship, so to speak; essentially a hierarchial system with himself at the top. Dr. Beu was inclined to loosen the structure in some ways, for the new President seemed to dislike the formality and rigidity which had been followed by his predecessor. He liked what he called the "open door" policy; a system which he once described to the Teachers College Board as follows:

> That is, the door to my office is literally open at all times. No secret meetings of any type are held at any time. If a student or faculty member requests a private conference, it is granted. Administrators not using the "open door" policy would be surprised how much it helps to overcome suspicion, jealousy, and stories based upon misinformation.[2]

While President Morgan seldom placed upon paper the extent of the educational philosophy to which he subscribed, a good deal was written by Dr. Beu which is quotable and which gives an indication of what he believed. In his inauguration address he said: "In teachers college we must give increased attention to the personal development of students. Our tendency has been to stress almost exclusively scholastic requirements."[3]

On other occasions he wrote of the profession of teaching. "Few teachers realize that a great deal of their difficulty with children may be due to the fact that they are not emotionally adjusted to the job at hand," he explained, "namely teaching." There is real "job insurance" in teaching, he continued, if the teacher does "all he can to see that those about him are happy."[4]

He had further ideas on the role of the teacher in the community. He once wrote for a professional journal: "The teacher should ordinarily conform to community traditions, standards, modes, and conventions, as far as possible." In the same article he added: "I want merely to emphasize that many teachers unnecessarily get into difficulty by trying to be clever in the classroom."[5] He wrote:

> Too many teachers talk shop about their students with other teachers and with persons in the community in general. This is a very poor practice, as it is not fair to the student to establish a halo effect concerning him; this halo effect is more often detrimental in character than it is beneficial.[6]

Looking back, it may be possible to state that Dr. Beu ran an informal, economical, and conservative school. His general policy involving advancement of the institution appears to have been bounded by a similarly conservative Board as well as by his own approach of asking for what he only thought he could get. This, plus his outlook upon certain extra-curricular activities of the school sometimes brought complaints from his faculty, not directly to him, but to the community in general.

Some faculty members felt that not enough was done for the instructional aspects of the school. Others felt that with the stress and strain brought on by increased enrollments, and the seeming emphasis upon athletic programs, that the standards of the school were undoubtedly suffering. It is probably true that both the critics and supporters of the policies of the administration after 1942 were not wholly correct.

Many members of the faculty welcomed Dr. Beu's relationships with them, and regarded them as refreshingly informal after the long years under Morgan. The new President was extremely devoted to golf—he still is—and gave a good deal of attention to the nine hole course added during his administration. He was, by nature, an early riser, and sometimes arrived on campus at dawn. To some he was a kindly man who was always doing little favors, some of them anonymously.

He appeared to have pet peeves, however, and one of them concerned the beauty of the campus, which he sincerely wanted to preserve. He waged an incessant war against man and beast alike in his desire to keep the grass untrodden.[7] He disliked waste and argued long and hard with his faculty to conserve the use of electricity. On one occasion he warned his teaching staff that they should use "lights as they would if they were paying the bill out of their own funds in their own homes."[8]

He seemed to have a great interest in athletics, and it is not surprising that the school had its greatest moments in sports during his presidency. He appeared to have a great pride in winning, and, to his faculty, he seemed to manifest a personal interest in the success of various athletes in the college. On occasion, he would be constrained to talk about the whole athletic program in faculty meetings, and when concerned about some particular aspect of sport, he wrote his advices for the college newspaper.[9]

II.

The problems with which President Beu was faced in 1942 seem in retrospect to have been insurmountable. Boys were leaving the campus in droves, and by the end of 1943 there were some 663 students and alumni in the armed forces.[10] The winter quarter of 1943 presented more sad news for the college when the total enrollment dropped to 382 students.[11]

Only the high demand for extension courses gave an excuse for the administration to hold faculty members in their positions. The faculty, in turn, actively solicited for students throughout the Military Tract and almost every high school in the area was visited by instructors from the college.[12] The slight increase in enrollment in the beginning of the academic year of 1944 brought no end to the problem. There were, as one girl put it, "no men;" an intolerable situation for the college as well as for the feminine sex.[13]

Even for the students who were enrolled, difficulties began to pile up. The establishment of Camp Ellis, a major army establishment a few miles away, created a crisis in housing faced by no other school in the teachers college system. Rents were high, and Grote Hall could handle only a portion of the demand upon it. President Beu was forced to contact house-holders personally in order to insure beds for incoming students.[14] He very likely had sufficient reason to complain that some householders near the campus were "using various schemes and devices" to evade rent controls established by the federal government.[15]

The academic year of 1945 brought new problems. Over forty names had been added to the "Gold Star" list of students and alumni killed in the service of the country, and every week seemed to add a casualty who was familiar to those who remained in Macomb.[16] When the war finally came to an abrupt end, Western counted its losses and faced the future with sober reflection. The prospects did not seem to present any optimism. "When World War II came to an end August 14, 1945," President Beu wrote, "I had visions of more normal conditions in administering affairs at the Western Illinois State Teachers College, but that is not the case. Today we have more problems. . . ." The college, he continued, had to solve the issue of housing which was an acute one; there were inadequate salaries paid to some instructors; and the college had to formulate an adequate building program.[17]

Because very little had been done to anticipate the first of these—the housing problem—enrollment figures placed an improper burden upon the already strained resources of the school. In 1946, 1200 students crowded into Sherman Hall for classes. Summer enrollment likewise increased and went to 1400 for both sessions in 1948. In 1951 the Fall enrollment shot to 1355, and in 1954 the *Courier* reported the number of students to be 1661. In 1956 enrollment went up to 2480, and in 1957 to 2605.[18]

Through all of this, housing was at a premium. President

Beu managed to acquire a number of old army housing units in 1946 and 1947, and these were located near the powerhouse, or near Lake Ruth, where approximately one hundred married people were housed.[19] Seal Hall, a dormitory for men, was opened in the spring of 1955, and an addition was added to Caroline Grote Hall. These measures took care of only part of the general demand, however, and housing remained as a pressing problem for the Beu administration.

III.

Despite the fact that the size of the student body fell to low levels during the war, Dr. Beu commendably fought to hold his faculty together, and the approximately eighty-two instructors were continued on the staff by reason of his effort.[20] It was much more difficult to hold the staff at the conclusion of the war, however, for the inflationary conditions of the post-war years wrought havoc with faculty incomes which had been static for some time. Employing new staff posed serious problems also. Dr. Beu complained in 1946 that he could not meet the higher salaries paid to faculty elsewhere. An English instructor employed for $330 a month at Western, for example, was lost to a New York college willing to pay $400. Various members of the faculty left for neighboring institutions capable of raising their salaries to livable incomes. Some who remained in Macomb found it necessary to supplement their insufficient salaries by other employment.[21]

Furthermore, faculty housing was at a premium. One faculty member, reported to be on a salary of $300 a month, reputedly paid almost one-third of that income for a three room unfurnished apartment. Another commuted from Galesburg fifty miles away, and others lived in nearby Colchester or Good Hope because they could not find suitable accommodations in Macomb. There were, in fact, several resignations because of this situation, and Dr. Beu asked the Board to consider the building of a faculty apartment house as well as a president's house in order to meet the emergency.[22]

By 1951 both of the problems of faculty housing and faculty salaries had been partially solved. A slight building boom in the town helped to ameliorate the first—along with more generous credit arrangement by local loan agencies. An increased understanding by the Teachers College Board served to relieve the second. By 1952 Western ranked second among the Board's college to Eastern Illinois State in the average salary paid to the professorial and associate ranks, highest in the rank of assistant, and third highest in the instructor category. The average salary in the top rank at Western for 1951 and 1952 was $6,241, and the other ranks were graded accordingly. It must be added that Western's fine position in terms of salary in 1952 was a temporary one. The President was forced to admit in the following year that the school had fallen behind; and throughout the 1950's the college found it most difficult to catch up with its sister institutions.[23]

IV.

Not only did the war have a profound effect upon the enrollment and faculty at Western, but it effectively prolonged the building shortage which had developed during the great depression. At the time of the economic collapse of the nation in 1929 few buildings were allowed to be planned for state college campuses because the state could not afford to pay for them. During the war years buildings were not constructed for more obvious reasons.

At the end of the conflict, however, rather expanded building programs took effect at other institutions within the state, particularly at the University of Illinois and Southern Illinois University, both schools being fortunate in having separate and independent boards.

President Beu's approach to a building program seems to

have been a conservative one, however. In his 1947 report to the Board he pointed out the need for certain additions to physical education facilities, the power plant, Caroline Grote Hall, and more acreage for campus expansion.[24] He eventually persuaded the Board to accept all of these proposals, plus other facilities suggested by himself in succeeding years. Grote Hall was extended to house more girls, and in 1949 the Teachers College Board approved the construction of a new football stadium in an extension of the ravine north of the school. This project was to be a self-liquidating one, paid for by students over a long period of time. It turned out to be a fairly well planned installation for the type of school which Western was at the time, and was opened to intercollegiate competition in 1950. Students and faculty were allowed to vote their opinions of a name for the place and, after a spirited campaign and much vented emotion, chose the name of Hanson rather than that of Champion or Beu.[25]

A rather expensive, but well built gymnasium addition to the campus training school was also part of the Beu program of expansion, and was soon opened to high school basketball competition. The library facilities, badly overcrowded as they were, received a slight palliative relief in the form of renovations providing some additional space. And a new golf course, the cost to be borne by monies from student fees, came into popular use. The President disclosed in his 1950 report that the rolling greens and broad fairway of the new golf course were in "very good shape." The swimming pool renovations were finally completed also, and were opened to general use in the early 1950's It need not be added, however, that little classroom space was provided by any of these additions.[26]

From the time of the completion of Sherman in the early years Western students had been plagued with odors and emanations from the chemistry laboratories located on the second floor. In 1951 the Board approved the construction of a new science building to be located to the west of Sherman Hall. The contracts for construction were let in 1953, and the building, now called Tillman Hall was dedicated in 1955. It was, from one point of view, an ordinary structure, but many felt then that certain economies were taken in construction which should not have been allowed. The building was very hot in the summer, air conditioning not being built into the structure, and soon the facilities seemed too small and overcrowded for the kind of program which the university needed to develop. Some years later air conditioning was added, but the building remained overcrowded until only recently.[27]

Slowly but surely the campus took on a new appearance through the 1950's. A shelter house was built on the golf course to take care of equipment as well as certain social activities planned for that area. As indicated before, Seal Hall had been dedicated in 1955, providing additional rooming space for Western men students. On the far western rim of the campus a new fine arts building was constructed after 1957, principally by reason of far-sighted interest on the part of the Board. It was, in fact, one of several such structures added to all of the teachers colleges located about the state. It is a multi-colored building which has large panels of varied hues and is now called Browne Hall.

At almost the same time a large combination student union and dormitory building was added to the campus near the Adams Street entrance. Consisting of two wings, one named Bennett Hall, the other Hursh, the structure truly relieved some of the housing pressures which had been build up in the past. The student union or lounge, as such, was a slight improvement upon past conditions, and it consisted of a snack bar with tables.[28]

V.

Along with some growth in the physical aspects of the campus, there was an enlargement of programs and curricula within the institution. Western, along with the other teachers colleges in the system, had flourished as an updated version of the normal school for many years. By 1940 there was some pressure, sometimes emanating from within the schools themselves, for a change in both name and status of each college. The barriers were first broken by Southern Illinois University, but others soon followed and Western was among them. In 1944 the Board approved the opening of graduate work in Macomb, and President Beu undertook an active part in pushing this program.

By the summer of 1944, graduate courses appeared in the catalog in such fields as elementary and high school methodology, school administration, chemistry, English, geography, mathematics, and social science. The first graduate degree granted by an Illinois teachers college was given by Illinois State Normal in 1945, but Western followed with a conferral within the year. Seven people received the M.Sc. in the summer of 1946, and the demand for graduate courses continued to mount. By the end of the year those doing graduate work had reached a significant figure, and the graduate school had become an essential part of the school's operation.[29]

Throughout the enlargement of faculty, facilities, and curricula, Western remained essentially a teachers college. This was true not only in regard to the attitude of administration and staff, but also in respect to appointments to the faculty. A liberal sprinkling of individuals holding methodology degrees, both on the doctorate and master's levels, was to be found in the so-called academic fields. Paradoxically, no Ph.D.'s in the academic fields were considered as instructors in methodology.

The administration became composed of those holding "education" degrees and it was apparently considered much more important how to teach than what to teach. In the latter part of the Beu administration, the impact of the space age began a token respect to research and writing; though one must stress the word "token." The method remained the medium; those who were trained in education still maintained the balance of power on campus.

Students were quite aware of this, and there were times when they made their feelings known. In 1947, partially due to student protests on the matter, the word "Teachers" was dropped from the title of the college. In the same year some nine hundred students petitioned the Board to allow the installation of a four year general college curriculum. President Beu backed this last cause, claiming that Western Illinois could be benefited by this kind of program. The Board turned him down, and it wasn't until 1957 that the same instrument of public authority granted an arts and sciences program to the University.[30]

One suspects that the astounding successes of the Russian space program had something to do with the 1957 innovation. Yet, long before the Board would recognize the need, the students yearned for a change in the concept of Western Illinois State College. It was the students who also yearned for an even broader interpretation of the 1957 ruling. As one student wrote:

> Maybe the situation could be remedied if courses other than English would require a student to read at least one book each quarter which would be considered in the intellectual category. The book would not have to be for English's sake, but could very well tie into the course through some particular aspect that went along with some phase of the subject.[31]

VI.

Campus life for the student in the Beu period was one of continued economic struggle. Housing was still in short supply in the late 1950's and students were forced to live in basements, attics, and cramped apartments. Many students lived on narrow budgets supported only by veteran allotment checks, or by wages earned by work in local factories. There were some similarities between student life in this decade and that of the depression years.

The Western student of the 1950's faced his weekend in differing ways. It was possible, though not probable, that he would have Saturday morning classes. A Saturday night dance sometimes held him in Macomb, as did fraternity or other responsibilities. All in all, however, most Western students were still weekend transients. In 1948, for example, almost one-half of the students deserted Macomb at the end of each week. Even married couples visited homes of parents or in-laws as a matter of practice.

There were several reasons for the weekend excursions. First, many of the students now owned automobiles, and these were used to bring food supplies from home to Macomb. Secondly, there were really few attractions on the campus, and not many more on the downtown square. The family at home was more likely to own television, and the home town was just as likely to have as adequate movies as those in Macomb.

Many students attended college during the late 1940's by virtue of teachers college scholarships and the "G.I. Bill." Among the freshmen of 1948 approximately twenty-five percent of the students were on a state scholarship, while twenty-two percent attended under the veterans' program. The sophomore class showed around eighteen percent on state scholarship, and forty-three percent under the "G.I. Bill." The percentages for the junior class were fourteen and sixty-two percent respectively, while in the senior class only eight percent were on state scholarships. Seventy-eight percent of the seniors were using veterans' privileges. In all, veterans composed about forty percent of the entire student body.

There are other interesting figures concerning the Western student in these years. The school was becoming of increasing economic importance to the business community which, until this time, had regarded the surrounding farm population as most important to its well-being. A 1948 survey indicated that fifty-seven percent of the single students of that year bought their clothes during the school year, and presumably in Macomb. Around eighty-two percent of the married students purchased their clothes within the school year. In the light of the times this amounted to a considerable source of revenue for the Macomb businessman. Single students, for instance, spent about two hundred dollars a year on clothing; an amount equalled by each married student.

School supplies represented an important category of student spending. Estimates indicated that thirteen to fifteen dollars per term were spent by students in bookstores in 1949. Beyond these slashes into the wallet came the rooming costs—five to eight dollars per week at the time. Board was an extra item in the budget, which accounts for so many of the young men and women of the immediate postwar era who did their own cooking. Costs for board in restaurants or boarding houses ran from twelve to thirteen dollars per week in some cases.

These seem rather small sums in view of costs per student today. The large dormitories virtually cut out personal preparation of food, which probably accounts for the fact that many students seek to find apartments whenever possible. Costs of books have gone up, and it is true that the number of books required for each course has multiplied.

A significant change in the post World War II years was in the presence or use of the automobile. About thirty percent of freshman students in 1948 owned cars, while sixty-seven percent of seniors were vehicle owners. Though the motorcycle has increased in numbers since 1948, it can be assumed that if the broad ownership of cars has not remained steady, it has increased somewhat.

The conclusions to be reached from the above figures are obvious. College life in the Beu period underwent tremendous changes and heralded the advent of the affluent college student of two decades later. The costs of a formal education were beginning to creep upward, for it was estimated that the average Western student spent fifteen hundred dollars a year; twice the amount two years earlier.[32] Thus did the new buildings, the increasing amounts of money spent by students, the growing size of the faculty, and the workers necessary to maintain the buildings bring an expanded prosperity to the Macomb area.

It is little wonder that the success of Western became a deep-rooted concern to the businessmen of Macomb. The size of the student body was duly noted in local newspapers, as well as the success of the athletic teams and the publicity attendant to the victories. This is not to say that Macomb was different in this respect, for like reactions were to be noted at Carbondale, Charleston, and DeKalb.

What it all meant in 1948 few people could really see. What it has come to mean is obvious. The American college is big business, and it will continue to become bigger.

VII.

The end of the war brought sweeping changes to the faculty at Western as well. Those who were Morgan appointees gradually began to retire. In 1948 the retired faculty still living included such names as Eva Colby, Bessie Cooper, Mabel Corbin, Irving Garwood, George Gaylor, R. M. Ginnings, Fanny Jackson, William Schuppert, Harvey Seal, Rupert Simkins, Alberta Strome, Katherine Thompson, and Walter P. Morgan. Ed DeCamp, who was the custodian of "old main" from the opening day, had retired in 1942.

One could not hope to mention all of the names of those who came to take the places of those listed above. Miss Margaret Donley and Mr. Loren Taylor joined the Academy staff in the early 1940's, and Dr. C. Adam Turner was an early Beu addition to the Education Department. Dr. Kent Pease returned from Red Cross service to sponsor the *Courier,* and Dr. Maurice

Myers joined the biology staff. Dr. Harriet Stull, Dr. Frances Whitehead, Mr. Paul Swain, Dr. Ruth Zimmerman, and Miss Lucille Neu were added to various departments. They were soon followed by Dr. Kenneth Goode, Dr. Loren Robinson, Dr. John McVickar, Dr. Dempsey Reid, and Dr. Forrest Wanninger.

In 1946 Dr. Robert Shiley replaced Garwood as the Head of the English Department, and a year later there appeared a number of new people who were destined to gain popular followings. These included Dr. Ogden Glasow, Mr. Kenneth Conn, Dr. H. W. Crall, Dr. Arthur Olsen, Dr. Victor Hicken, Dr. Reece Jones, Dr. Joseph Stipanowich, and Dr. Robert Ferguson.

Others of the "class of 1947" included Miss June Sebree, Mr. Robert Clow, Mr. Leroy Morley, Mr. Richard Abbot, Dr. William Lipsey, and Miss Nancy Neeley. Dr. Clifford Julstrom returned at the same time from graduate work. Among those coming in the years immediately following 1947 were Mr. George Mulder, Mr. Arthur Dufelmeier, Dr. Oren Gould, Dr. Wilma Warner, Mr. Leslie Van Etten, Dr. Roger Morrow, Dr. George Potter, Miss Marguerite Schormann, Dr. Dorothea Blyler, Mr. A. B. Roberts, and Dr. Olive Fite.

The outlook of many of these people was basically different than that of staff members a generation before. The faculty of 1934 was introspective, socially speaking, and strict interpretors of town and gown relationships. The new group readily mingled with people of the community. Furthermore, few of the new people, those of 1947, had doctorates when they came. These degrees were acquired not only through hard work, but at a good deal of financial sacrifice. Few of the 1947 newcomers owned cars, and many were forced to live in makeshift apartments. Despite these depressing situations, most of the people stayed on, becoming in time some of the more dedicated members of the faculty.

The motivation to obtain the doctoral degree was an inward one, for it would have been comparatively easy to have remained in the institution without such. It is true that there was mild pressure from school authorities to move up the educational ladder, but a look at statistics indicates that it must not have been great. In 1950 there were about thirty-four doctorates out of approximately 116 faculty members. Four years later there were thirty-five holders of the doctoral degree out of approximately 130 staff members.

The postwar years indicated important changes taking place in the administrative structure of the University. Mr. James Grigsby replaced Oscar Champion as the business manager, and Dr. Warren Covert became the principal of the training school. Dr. John Roberts replaced Rupert Simpkins as the Director of Placement and Training School, and Fred Currens retired in 1951 as the Dean of the College. Currens was replaced by Mr. William Lipsey who was doing work toward the doctorate at Northwestern University.

As the 1950's rolled by, there were further retirements and replacements. Miss Gladys Vawter retired from the English Department in 1954, and in 1956 Helen Pence, Dr. Arthur Tillman, Mr. Walter Eller, and Miss Isabel Hoover also went into retirement. In 1956 Dwight Bailey passed away, followed a year later with the quadruple loss of Louis Schleier, Chester Bennett, Mary Bennett, and Irving Garwood. Miss Theodora Pottle left the Art Department in 1957, Miss Hertha Voss retired as the Registrar, and Miss Beulah Mitchell left the training school. Mr. Roy Sallee left the active ranks in 1957; now able to continue his study of ant life unhampered.

It is interesting to note that three of the above individuals had been students at Western during its very early years. Miss Mary Bennett, Mr. Roy Sallee, and Miss Gladys Vawter had completed their first years of college training as freshmen students in Macomb. All three were popular college instructors, which speaks well indeed of the training which Western had given them.

The 1950's brought more than a score of newcomers to the staff. Dr. Jack Peterson joined the Education Department, Dr. Herman Griesenbrock came to industrial arts, and Mr. Howard Cordell was added to the library staff. Dr. Merle Lundvall and Dr. Paul Blackford were new additions to the English Department. Other additions included Dr. Arnold Wendt, Dr. Gifford Loomer, Dr. Luise Lenel, Miss Lois Mills, Dr. John Castle, Dr. Wendell Swanson, Dr. Donald Crawford, Dr. Forrest Suycott, and Dr. John Storey.

Some departments seemed to take on an entirely new look with the rapid enlargement of the staff. By 1957 the number of yearly appointments was so large that it was possible not to know a single person sitting around one at a faculty meeting. Indeed, with the growth of campus facilities, it was again possible for two old faculty friends not to see each other for several months at a time.[33]

VIII.

Through all of these years there existed within the faculty, and the student body, forces of contradiction and concern. Western was an easy going institution which seemed to have limited aims and interests. Scholarly pursuit might be present, but it was hard to find between the occasional and accidental mingling of the final exam week and national basketball tournaments. There were times during the latter episodes when it was not hard to notice that hundreds of students, and many of the faculty, were hundreds of miles away in Kansas City rooting for the team. Those who remained true to the cause of scholarship met in decimated classes back in Macomb. Life was certainly most informal, and the relationships between elements of the college community reflected this characteristic.

Still there were many members of the faculty who felt that there was misdirection of emphasis at the University. They tended to criticize the athletic program. Defenders of intercollegiate play pointed out that Western was only one of many colleges which sent teams to Kansas City; therefore, they said, there was nothing unusual in the practice. Attackers indicated a growing national need for effort along the entire educational structure, and argued that the country should place as much emphasis upon science as upon winning in this or that sport.

The answer to the whole controversy was given both here and elsewhere by a series of incidents. There were national scandals which involved big time gambling interests and so-called amateur sports programs. There were cheating episodes at West Point involving most of the football team. And there was the successful Russian attempt to orbit a space vehicle.

All of these events, plus the public sentiment of the time, were to radically affect the course of events at Western. In the late 1950's standards were considerably upgraded. There was an attempt to screen incoming students, and there was some mild encouragement given to faculty research. Western Illinois University was slowly coming of age.

IX.

One interesting aspect of campus life during the Beu period was the seemingly extraordinary number of faculty committees, committee meetings, and campus organizations taking up space on the University calendar. There were, in 1947 and 1948, some sixty social fraternities, sororities, and clubs in operation, with each student owing allegiance to several of them. Faculty members were called upon to advise these groups, as well as to take part in the duties of faculty government.

The faculty handbook of 1947 listed nearly forty faculty government committees; some of them important, some having no need for existence. The calendar of events for 1948 and 1949 listed close to 170 meetings of these various committees. This scheduled activity did not include committee meetings which resulted from emergencies.[34]

It is difficult to believe that the committee system became even more intricate later on. It was, as is easily seen, the continuation of the teachers college aura which surrounded the school. Despite the fact that the name of the institution was changed in the 1940's to Western Illinois State College (later popularly abbreviated to Western Illinois State), and that the name was again changed to Western Illinois University, the school retained the flavor of its normal school beginnings. During these same years, as now, there was considerable talk about students rating their instructors and helping in the determination of salary increases for individual teachers. That the system had failed during the Morgan period made little difference to proponents.

Beyond this evidence of small college thinking there were a great many facts to show that title changes notwithstanding, the school had changed very little in total philosophy. The Placement Bureau stated in 1950 that approximately two-thirds of the graduates of the college went into teaching. Three years later the percentage had increased to three-fourths. This fact alone indicated the nature of the school during the Beu years. The proof lay in the pudding, so said the old cliche, and the changes in the name of the institution had made little difference.[35]

X.

One of the substantial developments in the public image of the school occurred when the postwar flood of war veterans hit the campus. A 1946 survey pointed to the grades accumulated by these men and women, and there was some real pride in the increased intellectual effort which their presence aroused. In time the veterans left, however, and the old problems of striving to increase enrollments and of keeping students in order to improve the school's budgetary situation returned.

In the 1950's the fraternal and athletic activities gained

further attention on the Western campus.[36] There was, as is sometimes the case, some attendant bad publicity. Football games were forfeited by the playing of ineligible men, and reprimands were given to the school by the national athletic association to which the college belonged. These happenings served to hurt the school in many ways.[37]

There were other achievements, however. Mr. A. B. Roberts organized a full travel-study program, and soon the school had a national reputation for sponsoring such tours. By 1952 Western had sent travel groups to Cuba, New Orleans, Mexico, New England, Canada, the Northwest, Alaska, and to points in between. Soon Roberts had a world-wide tour program in operation, and Western's faculty members could be found all the way from Mandalay to Norway as leaders of such operations.[38]

By 1956 President Beu was the oldest of the Illinois teachers college presidents in point of service. He was beginning his fifteenth year as the leader of the institution. Few who had served the school through this period could say that their lives had been uneventful. From the unexpected three weeks vacation caused by the coal strike of 1950 through the last tortuous weeks of the Beu administration, the time had been a lively one. Rumors, faculty discontent, the honest efforts of a dedicated faculty, and a winter of discontent came to a culmination when President Beu retired.

Whether for or against, or pro or con, in the turmoil of the period, few faculty members and students could doubt the importance of the unexpected change at the helm. During the previous fifteen years the efforts of President Beu had brought some rather interesting alterations in the school. Now his retirement was an act which was designed to create many more.[39]

Chapter IX: *President Beu and the Beginning of Expansion*
1. *Macomb Journal,* June 19, 1942. According to the article, his dissertation was entitled: "The Legal Basis for the Organization and Administration of Publicly

Supported Normal Schools and Teachers Colleges in the Territory of the North
Central Association."

2. *President's Report to the Board,* 1954-1955.

3. *Macomb Journal,* Oct. 17, 1942; *Western Illinois St. College Quarterly,* Dec.,
1942.

4. F. A. Beu, "Emotional Maturity and the Teacher," *Illinois Education,* Sept.,
1942, p. 5.

5. F. A. Beu, "The Teacher's Ethics: A Guide to Successful Profession Relations,"
Illinois Teacher, Jan., 1937, p. 157.

6. *Ibid.*

7. *Courier,* Sept. 8, 1954.

8. *Ibid.,* Feb. 9, 1955.

9. *Ibid.,* Dec. 15, 1954.

10. *Annual Report of the President,* 1943-1944.

11. *Ibid.*

12. *Ibid.,* 1944-1945.

13. *Courier,* Sept. 20, 1944.

14. *Ibid.,* Sept. 8, 1943.

15. *President's Report to the Board,* 1943-1944.

16. *Courier,* April 24, 1945.

17. *President's Report,* 1945-1946.

18. *Courier,* Sept. 18, 1946; Sept. 20, 1954; Oct. 8, 1952; Nov. 1, 1957; *President's
Report,* 1947-1948; 1951-1952.

19. *Courier,* Feb. 5, 1947.

20. *Sequel,* 1944. This is my own tabulation.

21. *President's Report,* 1945-1946.

22. *Ibid.,* 1946-1947.

23. *Ibid.,* 1951-1952; 1952-1953.

24. *Ibid.,* 1946-1947.

25. *Courier,* Nov. 23, 1949; Dec. 14, 1949: *President's Report,* 1949-1950.

26. *President's Report,* 1949-1950.

27. *Courier,* Mar. 28, 1951; Nov. 18, 1953.

28. *Ibid.,* Oct. 7, 1953; Jan. 27, 1954; Sept. 25, 1957: *President's Report,* 1954-
1955.

29. *President's Report,* 1944-1945; 1945-1946.

30. *Ibid.,* 1948-1949; *Courier,* Sept. 11, 1957.

31. *Courier,* Dec. 11, 1957.

32. Lawrence C. Hackamack, *An Analysis of the Cost of Attending Western
Illinois State College,* June, 1948. This is an unpublished but thorough thesis
upon the subject of college costs at Western during this period.

33. The information concerning retirements, appointments, and administrative
positions comes from a general survey of college publications of the Beu era. I

know that I may have missed some names, and I apologize for the omissions.

34. *Faculty Handbook*, 1947; *Organization Calendar*, 1947-1948; *Faculty Committee Schedule*, 1948-1949. These are my own calculations.

35. *Courier*, Jan. 10, 1951; Dec. 16, 1953.

36. *Faculty Bulletin*, Nov. 14, 1946.

37. *Courier*, Oct. 27, 1954. Participation in post-season bowl games reputedly caused one of these reprimands.

38. *President's Report*, 1949-1950; 1952-1953.

39. *Courier*, Sept. 5, 1956.

CHAPTER X

President Knoblauch and Expansion

The early months of 1958 saw Western Illinois University undergoing a period of turmoil and dissent. The retirement of President Beu, plus deep and fundamental schisms within the faculty, combined to create a most unhappy time for much of the instructional staff as well as the students. Articles in metropolitan newspapers, plus a story in *Time,* heightened the intensity of feeling.

Each segment of the faculty blamed the cause for the school's plight upon the other. Only a few members of the staff pledged neutrality while waiting to sense the direction in which the University would go. Coincidentally, at the time of the culmination of the crisis, Walter Piety Morgan, long in retirement, passed away. The school, meanwhile drifted amid charges of incompetency and low standards on one side, and insinuations that one faculty element wished to create a "little Harvard on the Lamoine" on the other. As it was to turn out, neither side was to be wholly correct, and the institution righted itself through the aid of time and patience.

The Board, caught with some linens showing and yet cognizant to a degree of the situation in Macomb, attempted to meet the problem with some vigor. Dr. William Lipsey, Dean of the College, was given the additional task of managing the University until a permanent president could be named. After almost a month of continuing struggle with the unrest in Macomb, the Board allowed its Executive Secretary, Dr. Richard Browne, to assume the temporary presidency. For the next few months Dr. Browne traveled a rough road in attempting to act as the President of Western Illinois University while still remaining as Executive Secretary to the Board.[1]

Meanwhile, by a method hitherto successful at other institutions under its control, the Board set about to choose a suitable permanent president for Western. The faculty was allowed to elect by ballot a committee which, in turn, drew a limited number of possible candidates from the long list of applicants for the position. The smaller list, perhaps three or four in number, was then to be submitted to the Board. That agency was charged with making a final choice.

After a short but spirited campaign by various faculty groups, the committee was chosen. By May of 1958 it had completed its task, and the specified number of names was submitted to the Teachers College Board for its consideration. With little ado the Board settled upon the name of Dr. Arthur L. Knoblauch to be the next permanent chief executive of the school and, in the Fall of 1959, he was formally inaugurated as the President of the University.

Dr. Knoblauch's experience in educational administration had been long and interesting. He had won his baccalaureate at Michigan State University with a considerable amount of work in the field of agriculture. After some experience in the classroom he continued work on the master's level, and was granted an M.A. by the University of Michigan. His third degree, the Ed.D., came from Harvard University. Of the three schools, it was Michigan State which seems to have affected him most profoundly.

From then on in his life, Dr. Knoblauch led an eventful life both in the classroom and in administration. He became a Fulbright lecturer in Burma; an experience which probably accounted for his interest in the international aspects of education. After his return from the Orient he became the Director of Summer Sessions and University Extension at the University of Connecticut. As one would suspect, this program grew rapid under his direction.

From this position he was called to Moorhead State College in Minnesota as the President of that institution. His particular talents in building expansion were put to good use here, and Moorhead had a considerable growth under his leadership.[2]

It is no easy task to analyze the personality of such a man as Dr. Knoblauch. He is a very active type, and one may describe him as ubiquitous. He is seemingly mercurial in nature, his movements are deceptive, and his intelligence is acute. He appears to perceive the intent of questioning long before any would-be inquisitor arrives at the point of discussion He is a skillful debator, and can cleverly diffuse and obliterate the point of attack.

Yet, with all of these possible characteristics, he gives a sense of casualness. He is, in effect, a diversified man and seems to work hard at promoting this concept. He strolls more than he strides; he has an easy relationship with student and faculty, even though it is always on his terms; and he was often seen entering Sherman Hall with his overcoat lapels thrown back and his hands in his suit pockets.

One gained the impression in talking with him that he disliked discussions of petty quarrels among the staff. As the President he was patient but properly reluctant to enter into the minor problems of departmental struggles. Yet he was seldom unaware of difficulties within the school and he occasionally surprised the unsuspecting faculty member with his knowledge of them. He supported his department chairmen in the way in which they should be supported, and whenever he was forced to remove them he did so with a subtlety which gave solace to the unfortunate victim.

In essence, President Knoblauch was a builder. He was

profoundly interested in acquiring and constructing buildings for the university. He was successful in this, even though some of his faculty objected to the style or design which went into some of the structures. In the achievement of his building goals he was greatly helped by a substantial state bond issue act in the early part of his presidency, and a continuing public support for university growth until his retirement. It was characteristic of President Knoblauch to use the bond issue monies as quickly as possible so as to build what was necessary before the further inflation of the dollar.

One of President Knoblauch's initial moves was in the reorganization of the University administration. The office of the Dean of the College was almost immediately abolished and the duties of that post were incorporated into a theoretically more substantial position to be called Provost of the University. After sifting through applicants for this administrative post, President Knoblauch, with the help of a faculty committee, chose Dr. Earl Foreman of Moorhead, Minnesota.[3]

Dr. Foreman was a slender, dark haired man, who was genial and easy to talk with. His greatest asset was that he never seemed to be too busy to listen to the woes of instructors or department chairmen. This characteristic probably compounded his task, for the administrative duties assigned to him were rather enormous. His background, like Dr. Knoblauch's, was a varied one. He had attended Bradley University and the University of Illinois; the last institution the source of his Ed.D. For some years he had taught in Peoria and was, when picked to become Provost, a member of the Moorhead State College administrative staff.

A few words ought to be written about Dr. Foreman's devotion to duty. His office hours were regular, and he was seldom late. In poor health for some time, he continued to carry out his responsibilities in a way which many younger faculty members could not appreciate or understand. In the late months of his life he finally gave in and acquired an assistant dean, Dr. William Watts of the School of Business. The toll had been assessed, however, and in 1969 he was taken gravely ill. He died soon afterwards in an Iowa hospital and, in the tradition of Bayliss, Morgan, Van Cleve, and others, was buried in Macomb. Almost immediately his tact and skill were missed by all.

Other positions were created and filled by Dr. Knoblauch shortly after his arrival in Macomb. The office of the Dean of the School of Arts and Sciences went to Dr. H. Glenn Ayre, a tall, grey haired man who had been the Head of the Department of Mathematics. Dean Ayre had a record of publications behind him and his book, *The Basic Math Analysis of Junior and Senior Colleges,* had found wide usage throughout the nation.[4]

Dean Ayre's task was far removed from the continuing study of mathematics, however. The creation of a liberal arts atmosphere was, in a sense, out of the tradition of the University as a whole, and changes had to be wrought both gradually and subtly. Dr. Ayre trod his rather confined path of responsibility for a number of years, and did rather well under the circumstances before he retired from the faculty. As a post script it might be added that Dr. Ayre's interest in his field has not subsided and that he has published yet another book on mathematics.

After Dr. Ayre's retirement the office of Dean of Arts and Sciences remained virtually unfilled for some time; the faithful Dr. Foreman adding the duties of that position to his already overstressed schedule. Finally, after long deliberation by appropriate authorities, the post was filled by Dr. Winston Benson from Mankato, Minnesota. Dean Benson was forceful and vigilant about the powers of his office, but shortly after his appointment he resigned and returned to Mankato.

Again the position remained vacant for a time; that is, until Dr. Jay Stein, an experienced administrator from Iowa, was chosen by committee and appointed by the President as the new Dean of the School of Arts and Sciences.

The leadership of the Graduate Studies Program went to Dr. Julian Archer in 1959, shortly after Dr. Knoblauch's arrival. Dr. Archer was a kindly and forceful man who had taught in the Education Department since the early 1930's. He was "old school;" that is to say he believed in duty above all. His task of raising the level of graduate work at Western was filled with hazards and pitfalls, however, but he hewed to his principles. Unfortunately, in a few years, Archer fell ill and died suddenly of a circulatory ailment. In due time the post of Graduate Dean was filled by Dr. Henry Sather, for several years a member of the Biology Department.

Dean Sather is a phlegmatic and philosophic man; much the opposite of his predecessor. He desires expansion of the Graduate School while maintaining standards all along the line. One may suppose that with the substantial changes which are occurring in the Illinois educational system, Dr. Sather's position will become increasingly important.

Another of Dr. Knoblauch's administrative changes brought about the establishment of two more positions in the deans' category. These included the Dean of Public Services, an office originally designed to control public relations as well as summer sessions; and the Dean of Student Services, an office which placed under one director the older positions of the dean of women and the dean of men.

The first of the new administrative offices was filled by Dr. Carlson Crane, an easterner who had done academic work at the University of Connecticut where he had probably known Dr. Knoblauch. Dr. Crane's Ed.D. was granted by New York University.

The second position was taken over by Dr. John W. Henderson, just previously granted an EdD. by Michigan State University.[5] Henderson, unlike Dr. Crane, stayed only a few years then moved on to other positions—the presidency of Iowa Wesleyan College and the presidency of a university in Kansas. Henderson's place was taken by Dr. Gerhard Schwartz who came to Macomb from Mankato State College. Dr. Schwartz's Ed.D. was granted by Indiana University.

Another of Dr. Knoblauch's early appointments was that of Dr. Rolf Larson, who was given the position of Dean of the School of Education. Larson was an aggressive man, particularly in regard to the powers of the School of Education. Eventually he moved to a responsible position in the National Council For the Accreditation of Teacher Education, the headquarters of which were located in Washington, D.C.. Larson's replacewas Dr. Fred Abel, an affable and genial man whose doctorate was awarded by the University of Minnesota.

The magnitude of the changes brought about after Dr. Knoblauch's arrival were difficult for the faculty to grasp. As indicated previously, the number of doctorates in the Beu faculty approximated thirty-four out of 116 staff members in one particular period. By 1960 this figure had radically changed. A publication issued by the University in 1960 indicated that the number of doctorates had grown considerably, now totaling 103. In fact, the latter figure represented almost as many people as the entire teaching staff ten years earlier.

While the faculty several decades earlier had been fairly provincial in nature, the early Knoblauch faculty held doctorates granted by sixty-two different universities from all parts of the nation. Along with this interesting change came the establishment of the International Understandings Program, an idea pressed by Dr. Glen Westover which allowed foreign scholars to lecture at Western.

Within the first years of the Knoblauch era one could find a continuing widening in the offerings of the school. Thirty years previously there had been ten or eleven departments; now there were thirty-two. It was possible for a student majoring in education (the teacher training program) to do work in one of about eighteen different fields of study. There were twelve or more majors in the School of Arts and Sciences, as well as such pre-professional programs as those in dentistry, engineering, and law. A student might also work towards the M.A., the M.Sc., or the M.Sc. in Education. Later a six year program of advanced study in Education was added, and this seemed to be a sort of Pre-Ed. D. course before transfer to a larger university.

All of this represented a substantial picture of evolution. Yet, there were patterns of the past which persisted in the structure of the school. Western was principally a teacher training school, and it was administered as such. Furthermore, many of the popular departments of previous days still attracted most of the students. In 1959 a total of 373 students were awarded the baccalaureate. Fifty-nine of these went to business education majors, forty-nine were awarded in elementary education, and fifty-eight were given in physical education for men. For the first five years of the Knoblauch administration this particular tendency remained unchanged. In business education, for instance, the number of majors enrolled in both schools (Arts and Sciences and Education) totaled 431, while in 1961 it rose to 508.

Physical education for men enrolled 259 prospective majors in 1960 and 337 in 1961. Its rate of growth, in proportion to the population of the University, fell off after 1965. Home Economics also began to lose in the percentage race for students. In the 1930's it was one of the most popular departments in the college. In the 1960's there were increases but not major ones.[6]

To those whose lives were inextricably entangled with the fate of the University, the pattern for the future seemed to be one of numbers. In 1960 the colleges and universities of the state were hit by the first wave of "war babies." The increased building, brought on by bond issue legislation, posed a greater temptation for the colleges and universities operated by the State of Illinois to solicit more students. By 1966 it was obvious that university growth was correlated in some quarters with university quality, and that a college education was now viewed rather as a birthright than a privilege. Furthermore, the enlargement of the Viet Nam War served to spur the enrollment of young men in colleges, for this was one way of postponing the military draft.

An important development of the 1960's was the growing acceptance of the principle of "self-liquidating" dormitories. The idea involved here was that the buildings would be built on borrowed money, and that the debt would be paid off by the students who lived in the dormitories. Not only did this force the colleges and universities into semi-coercion in pressing the students to live in dormitories, but it forced the same institutions to apply all measures necessary to keep the buildings occupied. Thus began a dilemma in the round; the colleges built self-liquidating dormitories, and then found it necessary to ask the General Assembly for more money for classroom buildings and instructors.

II.

Years before, it had been obvious to students and faculty alike at Western that the most crying need of the school was a new library. Nearly fifty years ago the *Courier* stated: "Western needs a new library building with modern equipment including two or three spacious reading rooms, a separate room for periodicals, an office for the librarian, and plenty of space for stacks and files."[7]

A new library was opened in 1962, and the students and faculty joined in so that books might be moved into the structure. Unfortunately, by the time the new building was completed, the space was already inadequate. Called the Memorial Library, it was poorly located for the decade to come, and too much room was given over to facilities not remotely connected with the storage of books. The upper floors were given to the audio-visual and radio services of the University and, on the very top, there was constructed a lavish reception room which was of little use to the student interested in reading and research.

It is possible that a little foresight concerning growth might have avoided the mistakes in the construction of the new Memorial Library. By 1960 the University already had Caroline Grote Hall and Mary Bennett Hall for women, and Seal Hall and Hursh Hall for men. Washington and Lincoln dormitories were soon on the drawing boards, and President Knoblauch was predicting that by 1970 there would be 5200 students enrolled at Western. The actual figure would be over twice that at the end of the 1960's, and would possibly be as much as 24,000 by 1980.

The President was understandably wrong in early prediction of growth, for he could not have known what the total effects of bond issue construction would be. As soon as the 1960 bond revenue money was made available, Dr. Knoblauch did set in motion a huge expansion program. He planned $14,000,000 in new buildings, including an applied sciences building, a physical education building, a health center, a new campus school, a classroom building, a new greenhouse, and other smaller structures. Work was commenced as soon as permission was granted by the Board, and the University began to grow.

The impetus given to university construction by bond issue money continued long after the original funds were spent. Another classroom building, for mathematics and social sciences, was constructed on the "north" campus. A life sciences building, perhaps the most impressive structure on the campus, went up in the same area. Ground was broken for a handsome building to house the new School of Business, and for another structure in which to quarter the chemistry and physics departments.[8]

Meanwhile Higgins Hall, a dormitory for women, was built over the west side of the old golf course. It is "high rise," and tends to dominate the portion of the campus in which it is built. A similar dormitory, called Thompson Hall and located north of Higgins, was gotten underway in the late months of the Knoblauch administration. By April of 1967 President Knoblauch was able to say that, during his tenure in office, Western Illinois University had spent over $50,000,000 in new construction.

To some of the faculty there were seeming contradictions, however. While the School of Business retained a growth and totaled about 1350 majors in 1969, thus being entitled to a new building, other areas of study had fallen off. The School of Applied Sciences, created in the second half of the Knoblauch era, handled 2230 students in the fall of 1968, and yet was housed in one of the finest buildings on campus. This number was less than such individual departments as history (2417 students) and mathematics (2633 students), both of which were located in Morgan Hall along with sociology and philosophy (1453 students) and political science (1800 students). A similar condition was to be found in physical education for men, which was listed as having 421 majors in the 1967-1968 year; a growth of less than 100 in the previous decade. The redeeming factor in the new and expensive building for the School of Health, Physical Education, and Recreation was that the structure did serve a great number of activities—graduation ceremonies, service courses in physical education for men, etc..

Meanwhile something was happening to the old liberal arts fields. History as an area of study surpassed physical education for men in terms of majors, and almost doubled the number of physical education majors among the women. Mathematics continued an upward spiral. Political science was beginning to bulge at the seams, while sociology was gaining rapidly in popularity. English, as shall be pointed out below, quadrupled the number of majors in physical education for men.[9]

As the new buildings went up, the functions of older ones began to change. Sallee Hall, a bond issue building, was given over to a foreign language and other fields, while the English Department moved into Simpkins Hall, a renovated version of the old training school. The old "fine arts" building, constructed in the Morgan era, awaits a dubious future, while Sherman Hall has gone almost completely to an ever increasing administrative staff.

One of the great additions to the campus during the Knoblauch era was the University Union Building. The original building was opened in 1964 at a cost of $2,000,000, and it included a cafeteria, meeting rooms, a bowling alley, and a snack bar. In September of 1968 a $3,500,000 addition was completed, which made the building one of the more attractive student facilities in the state. Rooms for campus visitors, a bookstore, a "Grand Ballroom," various meeting rooms, the Prairie Lounge, a billiards room, the Mississippi Room, and the Sandburg Room were some of the new attractions in the building. The total footage of the enlarged University Union was 185,000 square feet, and it was estimated that between 10,000 and 14,000 people entered the building each day.[10]

All of this amounted to a fantastic building program and President Knoblauch pressed it vigorously forward. Still, it is obvious that the University will soon exceed 15,000 students and that what was feasible today may not be applicable tomorrow. The rapid shifting of students from one field to another, the changing motivational aspects of student life, the impact of the junior college system in the state, and the struggling nature of the Graduate School still present problems. There are also some departments who are already being overwhelmed by the torrent of students. Somewhere along the line of growth, it seemed necessary for the University, Western that is, to pause and attempt to understand the wave of the future.

III.

One of the important changes in respect to Western's faculty had to do with real income. The changing attitude of the public toward education and with respect to teachers' salaries was a nationwide one, and it resulted partially from a sympathetic news media as well as from the activities of teachers themselves. Though President Knoblauch hastened to improve the lot of his faculty in terms of salary, he was in truth acting in concert with conditions of the time.

One major impulse in the promotion of higher teacher income was provided by "sputnik" in the late 1950's. Another was the very real shortage of high school and college instructors brought on partially by the rapid increase in school-age population. A college in Iowa, for example, advertised in the mid-1960's for a teacher of history with a specified annual income of $30,000. These dream conditions were not realized at Western, but the increases in salary conditions were substantial. The mean salary of the staff in 1957 was $6600, but by 1965 it was up to $9752. As it continued to move upward, many of Western's instructors were able to live on the level of many other professional people in the town.[11]

It must be added, however, that the very teacher shortage served to dampen the median increase in salaries from 1965 on. It was not easy to employ doctorates, and furthermore the influx of students into the lower division courses caused the administration to bring in larger numbers of instructors in the "A.B.D." category (all but doctorate). While salaries did continue to increase, the fact that Western's faculty became increasingly younger and increasingly within the instructor's rank brought the median increase down somewhat.

Through the entire decade of the Knoblauch period there were deaths among retired faculty as well as a continued steady retirement of older members of the instructional staff. Mabel Corbin and Fred Currens, both long retired, died in the academic year of 1959-1960. Harold Schory retired during the same period and passed away a few years later. Dean Julian Archer died while still in service, and Roy Sallee, who had previously retired, died in 1964. Ruth Carson, formerly Head of the Foreign Language Department, died in 1966. She had been preceded in death by the former Dean of Women, Dr. Ruth Zimmerman.

Other retirements included Ray Hanson, Grace Sproull, Lyndall Swofford, Juna Reynolds, Glenn Ayre, and Sarah Miner. Dr. Robert Shiley retired and moved to Chicago. Dr. Kathleen Brophy, after whom the women's physical education building is named, also retired and spends her year in Florida, Macomb, and the upper Michigan peninsula.

It would be impossible to name all of the additions to the staff during the Knoblauch period. There were some changes in upper administrative personnel and these should be noted. Dr. Richard Gibb, previously in the Department of Agriculture, rose to a vice-presidency in the institution, but he left for an administration position in another state when President Knoblauch retired. Mr. James Grigsby was named the Vice President for Business Affairs; a position which he richly deserved. Dr. Howard Nudd was named as Dean of the School of Business, and Dr. Harry Fritz was given the post of Dean of the School of Health, Physical Education, and Recreation. Dr. Franklin Pierce Gardner was appointed as the Dean of the School of Applied Science, and Dr. Forrest Suycott was named as the Dean of the School of Fine Arts. One of Dr. Knoblauch's last acts was to appoint Dr. John G. Westover as the Dean of International Services.

IV.

The 1960's began in a spirit of mild national despondency. The "cold war" between Russia and the United States had

intensified, particularly after the U-2 affair and the collapse of
the Paris Conference between President Eisenhower and Pre-
mier Khrushchev. The election campaign between Senator
John F. Kennedy and Vice-President Nixon, though spirited,
brought forth charges from the former that there was a widening "missile gap" between Russia and the United States. This
charge was far from true and, as it turned out, it fell into the
vein of campaign oratory.

Nevertheless, all of the talk about growing Russian strength
in missiles served to depress many Americans. In September of
1960 President Knoblauch, addressing the parents of new students, stated: "We make no predictions when, if ever, the next-
all-consuming war may reduce us again to the stone age, but we
do want to express the hope that it won't be for the next four or
possibly six years."[12]

Despite the gloominess of prevailing sentiment, the months
and years rolled by with no atomic holocaust. Senator Kennedy
defeated his opponent in 1960 by several eyelashes and the big
city vote, and the missile gap mysteriously closed. Richard M.
Nixon, down but not out, prepared himself to follow Arnold
Toynbee's principle of "withdrawal and return." And President
Knoblauch proceeded on his course of change and evolution at
the University, apparently operating on the assumption that the
nation was good for another decade or two.

True, the Dutch elm disease wiped out virtually all of
Macomb's most stately trees; but on the other hand the Sherman
Hall bells were fixed, thus presaging some hope for the future.

Nevertheless, there remained in some parts of the administration a concern about the possibility of atomic war. An alarm
siren was installed in the center of the campus, but unfortunately its initial trials were fiascos since it was wrongly installed
and ran backwards. Little hand drawn descriptions of escape
routes appeared on the bulletin boards of each classroom, with
the route of departure outlined in yellow. There was even talk

that Sallee Hall, a windowless building, had been built as much for an air raid shelter as for a classroom building. Administrative officers argued that this was a wrong assumption, and that the lack of windows allowed for a conservation of heat in winter and a better functioning of air conditioning in summer.

All in all, however, Sallee Hall was, in the beginning, a depressing place in which to teach. Sounds reverberated from all parts of the classrooms, and the voices of instructors were difficult to hear. And, contrary to the purported plan, many of the rooms were cold in winter, and dampish and warm in summer. It soon became obvious that Sallee Hall might be the last windowless college classroom building at Western. The campus school, soon under construction, likewise lacked windows. The qualification here was that it was not for college classes or college type instruction; even though air-conditioning difficulties made teaching conditions there as difficult at times as they had been in Sallee Hall.

The Knoblauch period heralded broad changes in student life at Western. The old Vet's Village, a set of shacks located near Lake Ruth, was torn down and replaced with Corbin Hall. Despite the commencement of dormitory construction, a large part of the Western student body still lived in private housing facilities. University authorities indicated in 1960 that over 1300 students rented rooms or apartments and while many in the administration sought to cut this number considerably, it was freely admitted that students who lived outside the dormitories had more "fun."

With the continued construction of new dormitories, however, enrollment in the University began to soar. By 1963 there were 4942 students (counting campus school enrollment), with the freshman class amounting to 2248 of this total. Survey level classes were strained to the ultimate, and some departments attempted to go to mass lectures with varying measures of success. Students, in general, disliked the large sections, and so did the teaching staff. All in all, a condition was created in the University which led some of the faculty to feel that Western had become a junior college, and that true university growth would be severely hindered. This may have been true for, while Northern Illinois University and Illinois State University soon moved out from under the Board of Governors, Western and Eastern remained under that agency with two Chicago colleges.

In 1963 a married student housing project was added to the campus, being built near the top and east side of the old ravine. Though it housed only twenty-eight couples, it managed to alleviate housing difficulties encountered by married students.

The influx of students to Macomb, and the growth of the University during the 1960's, had a profound effect upon the town's development. Private housing investors soon saw the possibilities of profit in the construction of apartments and homes for faculty and students. A housing boomlet started, first to the west of the University in the Currens' addition, and then out in a section along the Lamoine River called Riverdale. Speculators built apartments on Adams and Charles streets, and plans were drawn for more apartment buildings elsewhere in town. Western Illinois University had become big business, as Dr. LeRoy Donaldson discovered in a 1964 study of student expenditures in Macomb. It was estimated that almost a million dollars had been spent in the town by Western students during the spring quarter of that year.

Yet, the cost of attending Western Illinois University remained fairly low by comparison to other Illinois institutions. In 1960 it was shown that students could get by on $365 a quarter (probably including tuition), and that yearly costs barely exceeded $1000. A few years later, after some inflation had occurred, the University estimated that a student could attend the school on less than $1400 a year (on a bare minimum).

Everything was to spiral upward in ensuing years, however.

The increasing inflation, plus greater numbers of students, brought attendant results in the community. Snack stands sprang up along the main arteries of traffic. Pizza parlors, hamburger stands, and frozen dessert places made their appearance along West Jackson Street. And Adams Street, just off the campus, fell victim to the times with new bookstores, a drugstore, and other businesses opening to fill the students' needs. Parenthetically, the square uptown fought to maintain its portion of student business by providing, for a while, free bus service for students to that part of town.

There was an increasing broadening of the whole educational spectrum within the University as well. The lecture and entertainment program was enlarged, and Mrs. Eleanor Roosevelt and the Philippines diplomat Carlos Romulo came to the campus in 1959. Woody Herman, a jazz clarinetist, appeared in 1960 as did the St. Louis Symphony Orchestra. The University Union served to make such offerings more attractive; even though the first entertainer to appear in this building was Mr. Max Morath, a ragtime piano virtuoso. The visiting lecturer program, inaugurated and carried on by Professor Westover, brought to the Union speakers from India, Hong Kong, Japan, Malaysia, Turkey, the United Arab Republic, Great Britain, Austria, Greece, and Mexico.

There also appeared on campus at this time a group of Nigerian students. Brought here under auspices of a Federal program, they added a certain fillip to life on the campus. They provided the best players for a thrown-together soccer team, and all in all they were excellent students. They were also ambitious and could be seen at local banks at the end of each month depositing stipends sent to them from Washington.

While many American universities flavored their student bodies with foreign students, it remained for most to offer the same kinds of opportunities to American Negroes. It was estimated, for instance, that there were more foreign students in

American universities in 1968 than American Negro citizens. Though this condition was not as bad at Western (the percentage of American Negroes at Midwest universities has always been higher than elsewhere), it must be written that a good deal of concern was given to the recruitment of foreign students and foreign faculty members in administrative circles.

The opening of Corbin Hall in 1962 offered a new level of living for many of Western's women students. Called the "Corbin Hilton" by some, it was boasted that each floor was equipped with a lounge, a typing room, and a shampoo room. Also located about the building were laundry rooms equipped with both washing and drying machines.

The new dormitories caused a minor social change on the Western campus. Fraternities and sororities began to decline in significance. And the girls who lived in the new buildings added a new nuance to spring and summer. They sunbathed in the open, particularly on a plot of ground near Adams and Western streets. Since bathing suits became scantier during the 1960's the University sought to avoid the embarrassment of passing motorists with the construction of a wooden fence. This was useless, for the girls spilled beyond the confines of the fence and ever nearer to the road.

All of the new dormitories severely tested the moral codes of the past. The tendency of the University to force dormitory living, especially upon first year students, took the girls from under the protective hands of housemothers in private housing and in sororities. One of the more obvious results was daytime "petting;" a practice which offended the sensitive eyes of the older generation. Even the *Courier* had a few words to say about the behavior of such students. "Public displays of affection are not ever in good taste," it stated, "and can be especially shocking to visitors and parents."[13] The paper might have also added that rarely, if ever, did a girl who acted thusly last in the University more than the academic year.

V.

There were moments and events to remember in the Knoblauch era, and some of them are bound to be indelibly etched into the minds of students of that time. In 1959, for instance, one of Western's finest football teams was fielded; a squad which included such men as Warren Dew, Leroy Jackson, Booker Edgerson, and Dan Washkevich. The team was so good that many of the players were immediately snatched up by professional teams in the two major football leagues.

There was another occasion when the water supply in Macomb fell to disastrously low levels. The University supposedly went on emergency rationing for a short time, though it was rumored that some of the more prominent faculty members were sprinkling their lawns after dark. But the city struggled through the crisis with the aid of the Lamoine River, and students were once again allowed to bathe.

A day to remember was November 22, 1963, when President John F. Kennedy was killed by an assassin's bullet. Assassination was an act which did not seem possible in contemporary America. The deed was first heard with disbelief, then shock, and lastly with a sense of bewilderment and loss. It is not an exaggeration to say that students and faculty struggled to keep their composure through the remainder of that day. Nor did the weather help. The rain continued to fall, and the day passed by with a greyish pall which is peculiarly midwestern.

President Knoblauch did not immediately dismiss classes, but some instructors could not go "onstage" and appeared only to tell their students to go home. By three o'clock Sherman Hall was almost completely deserted, while most students and faculty gathered around television sets in order to watch the dreadful proceedings.

But the shock of assassination was an emotional upheaval to which Western students were to become accustomed. Martin Luther King's death in Memphis caused the administration to hold a memorial service in the Multiple Purpose Building, and Robert Kennedy's death was another catastrophe to be endured. The last murder caused the least reaction in the Western student body. It was not that most students did not feel strongly about the event, but rather that the nation's entire nervous system had already been emotionally drained.

President Knoblauch retired in 1968 as the President of Western Illinois University. There were the usual farewells and dinners which are given to a retiring president, plus the President's last two commencements. During the spring graduation ceremonies Dr. Knoblauch was the speaker of the day. In an address entitled "The Crisis in Our Culture," he outlined what he thought were the fundamental problems of the day. He said in effect that American society had lost its moorings, and that "this generation doesn't suffer from anything that my generation hasn't recovered from and mastered."

For anyone who had studied the nature of American students in general in 1968, the President had said indirectly what many Americans were saying. Ensconced in their massive dormitories, with plenty to eat and warm lodgings, the students had come a long way from the outdoor toilet and the oil lamp. While many of their faculty had endured through one terrible war, the vermin of veterans' housing, and the difficulties of making financial ends meet, it was very likely that few of the new breed had ever seen death or birth or had suffered very long from the pangs of hunger. That, for the elder generation, was the real meaning of a generation gap. To the younger, however, it was a story too often repeated and lost in its meanings.

In his final speech the President tried to relate to many of his faculty, and to the students, the innermost thoughts of a man deeply troubled. Perhaps speaking to the younger generation, he said:

> Today our philosophers have lost their philosophical moorings.
> They discuss and analyze and criticize what is, and they forget

that most of us are going to spend our time in the future. They question the values of the past and of another day, but they offer nothing new—either tried or untried.[14]

There is little question that the University had come a long way under Dr. Knoblauch. The postage stamp campus had grown into a large and attractive complex of buildings. The student body had become so large as to be almost depersonalized. The faculty had become massive by comparison to what it had been. Some departments had grown too rapidly; some too slowly. But those were only a part of the continuing problems of any institution. The Knoblauch era, with its signs proclaiming the virtues and sources of each building on campus had now come to an end.

Chapter X: *President Knoblauch and Expansion*

1. *Courier,* Feb. 26, 1958.

2. *Ibid.,* May 14, 1958.

3. *Ibid.,* Sept. 10, 1958.

4. *Ibid.,* Dec. 14, 1949.

5. *Ibid.,* Dec. 10, 1958.

6. Information from the Registrar, 1961; also from Office of Institutional Planning and Development.

7. *Courier,* Feb. 13, 1926.

8. *Courier,* Feb. 15, June 28, 1961.

9. Information from Office of Institutional Planning and Development.

10. University Publication, *Staff,* June 6, 1969.

11. *Statement of Request For Preliminary Accreditation of the Certificate of Advanced Study in Educational Administration Program,* written for Commission on Colleges and Universities of the North Central Association, Western Illinois University, Macomb, Illinois, 1967.

12. *Courier,* Sept. 7, 1960. President Knoblauch may have been speaking in jest.

13. *Ibid.,* Jan. 24, 1962. Dr. Donaldson's study appeared in *Courier,* June 3, 1964.

14. "The Crisis in Our Culture," by Dr. A. L. Knoblauch, published by Western Illinois University Press, 1968.

CHAPTER XI

A New President For Western

During the summer of 1968, a faculty committee conducted a diligent search for a successor to President Knoblauch. Candidates from Texas, California, and Virginia were interviewed, but the choice finally settled upon Dr. John T. Bernhard who came from Utah. In the Fall of the same year the new President was installed in office.

President Bernhard's life shows a broad and interesting background. He was born in New York, but heeded Greeley's purported call to go west. In the year of the Pearl Harbor disaster he was granted a B.S. by Utah State University; an institution which is known for giving its graduates the inspiration to attend graduate school. Following the war President Bernhard was granted the M.A. and Ph.D. by the University of California at Los Angeles. It might be noted here that Dr. Bernhard is the first president of Western to have obtained the doctorate from outside the field of pedagogy.

Dr. Bernhard's war years were spent as an anti-submarine officer in the United States Coast Guard Reserve. Following his discharge he obtained a position at Logan Senior High School in Utah. His teaching experience here was brief for in 1947 he became a teaching assistant and lecturer at U.C.L.A., where he continued his graduate work. Following the winning of the doctorate he was employed as an assistant professor at Brigham Young University. He left that position in 1951, however, when he took a position as a staff assistant to Howard R. Hughes, the well known financial wizard. In 1954 Dr. Bernhard again moved, becoming a commodity research analyst in North Hollywood, California.

He returned to the educational field in 1959 by becoming the administrative assistant to the president of Brigham Young University. The rise upward was thereafter quite rapid. He was named the Dean of Humanities and Social Sciences at B.Y.U. in 1962; a position which eventually evolved into the Dean of Social Sciences. In 1966, while on leave from B.Y.U., on a Rockefeller Foundation grant, he began an advisory task at the Federal University of Minas Gerais in Brazil. Shortly after his return to Brigham Young he was called to Western Illinois University to assume the presidency.

Having done his graduate work in political science, it was natural enough for Dr. Bernhard to engage in some political activity in Utah. He was a state senator for four years, and served on various commissions and legislative councils related to state governance.

Long before all of these achievements he was married to Miss Ramona Bailey of Logan, Utah, in 1941. She is an attractive and courteous lady and the mother of four children.[1]

Though President Bernhard's administration is relatively new, he has made a few of his beliefs known to both students and faculty. On September 11, 1968, in an address to the faculty, he indicated his firm insistence in the concept that the faculty is the "central core of any university." He spoke of the need for long range planning, and of the so-called "Master Plan" for the development of higher education in Illinois.

Furthermore, he informed his listeners that, in his view, the president should be *primus inter pares,* and he stressed the point that a president should rarely take unilateral action in areas of concern to the faculty. It probably came as a shock to many of Western's faculty that the new President was to be

only the first among equals for tradition, relationships with the
Board, and associations with the growth of the University make
this a difficult aim to achieve.

Speaking in a general sense he informed the faculty that
recent years had eroded the traditional relationship between
students and their faculty. To support this view he quoted from
a Brookings Institution survey as follows:

> There is a whole generation of able young faculty members who
> never knew a time when affluence did not prevail. Thus it is
> hardly surprising that a few of them exhibit an opportunism that
> startles their elders. Some of these heavily-bid-for young people
> appear to have no sense of institutional loyalty whatever, and
> simply follow the offers where they lead.

This remarkable speech of September, 1968, served to point
up what a great many older teachers had already noted; that
the tremendous growth of American education had drawn into
the teaching profession a number of individuals who were attracted by the prospects of personal gain. Few had gone through
the lean years; indeed few were ready to contribute to the reputation and tradition of selflessness which teachers of the past
had built up. "He who has no vision has not yet lived," stated
Dr. Bernhard. And as for students, the President said: they are
sometimes regarded as impediments to high salaries, grants, and
publishing ventures to be won by many young instructors.

One week prior to his address to the faculty in 1968, President Bernhard presented a sampling of his views to the freshmen of 1968, or the Class of 1972. He spoke feelingly of his intensity of emotions in becoming the President of Western Illinois
University, and related these to the attitudes of new students.
He challenged the students to think about their futures, and
what they wished their careers to be. "Character development,"
he argued, was one of the most important aspects of student
life. "Don't be confused by the upheaval;" he told the students, "don't be misled by the shrill and strident cries for 'in-

stant reform or else. . . .' " Furthermore, he warned, one must "never lose sight of the cultural depth of our heritage."

The President concluded this address with a stricture that students should not be guilty of "thinking with one's blood. . . ." "Honor" and "integrity", "right and wrong", and principles were still character landmarks to be followed in one's relationships with another.[2]

II.

President Bernhard had inherited a school which, in 1969, indicated both problems and promise. The total number of students had increased from the 1964-1965 term average of 5172 to the 1968-1969 term average of 9461. The difficulties raised by this growth were of a significant nature. The percentage of lower division students had remained far too high, and hindered the development of upper division instruction. In 1965-1966, for instance, the lower division students approximated seventy percent of the student body. By 1968-1969 the percentage of lower division enrollees had dropped somewhat, but it still amounted to well over half of the student body.

While this did not serve to block the maturation of some departments, others which had the obligations of large service course enrollments found it necessary to adjust accordingly. Particularly was the impact felt in the School of Arts and Sciences. In the Fall of 1968, the English Department conducted 207 undergraduate classes with a total enrollment of 5557 students. This burden was handled by an English staff of sixty-one instructors. The History Department of the same school taught 2417 students with 20.25 instructors, and the Political Science Department instructed 1800 students with 13.10 instructors.

The effect of these burdens can be seen in the graduate level instruction carried on by the three departments during the same term. English conducted six classes of the 500 level or better with a total of forty-two students. History had only one 500 level class with ten students, and political science shepherded ten students through three classes.

Yet other departments were relatively unaffected by the lower division surge. The Department of Education, in Fall of 1968, taught 2079 undergraduate students with 34.66 faculty members (see history figures above). Its departmental graduate offerings were open to 423 students in thirty different sections; some of them taught as extra loads in the extension division. Biological Sciences handled 1705 undergraduate students with 23.25 staff members, while it taught eleven 500 level courses or above with sixty-four students. The same disparities showed elsewhere in facts and figures gathered by the University's Office of Institutional Planning and Development.

In terms of growth, some departments had shown a tremendous surge in numbers of majors. The English Department, in the Fall of 1968, tabulated 1649 majors, while History approached the 600 mark. Geography and Geology, while having 21.33 instructors, listed only ninety-nine majors. Home Economics, while still growing, was not carrying the same percentage of majors among the total student body as it had during the 1930's. In the Fall of 1968 that department listed 327 majors with 16.10 faculty members. The Department of Physical Education for Men also indicated a slow growth with 497 majors with 23.80 staff members. In 1961 the same department had 337 majors.

One of the important changes in the previous ten years had been the tendency to grant academic status to non-teaching administrative University personnel. One must hasten to point out that the development of such a practice at W.I.U. was in accord with conditions elsewhere in the country. A cursory examination of the 1961 *Sequel*, which was published in the Spring of that year, shows about 160 people in the instructional area. In the following Fall the academic staff was numbered at

237. One must assume that, with the increase of instructional staff over the previous spring and other factors, the number of non-instructional academic staff was small.

By 1968 the situation had changed. The Office of Institutional Planning and Development, in June of 1969, indicated that out of the sum total of 673 academic employees, only 498.5 were actually involved in instructional duties. There may be solid explanations for this, but the figures seem to show a tendency to cover a burgeoning office personnel with the academic blanket. They also show that the administration of a university is no longer a simple task, and that it must be delegated to growing numbers of people. Western had come a long way from the time when President Henninger was the registrar, chief executive of the school, and athletic director all rolled into one.

III.

One of the duties of non-instructional staff personnel is to provide the University with information about itself. Some of that information which relates especially to students is quite revealing.

First, it must be pointed out that no longer does the University depend solely upon the old Military Tract for students. Cook County, for instance, will probably send nearly 3000 students to Western in the Fall of 1969. This will be twice the number sent by that county to the school in 1965.

DuPage and Rock Island Counties are also now the sources of many in the school's student body. The first has almost doubled its 1965 total and is now nearly 700; the latter is nearly 400.

Yet, it must be pointed out that McDonough County still accounts for approximately 600 students, and that Fulton, Schuyler, and Hancock Counties are important contributors to the University's growth. Almost every county in the state is

represented in the student population; the exceptions being
Gallatin, Hamilton, Lawrence, and Pulaski. Gallatin is a very
poor county in the southern tip of the state, and the other
three tend to send their students to state schools nearer to their
locations.

While it is true that Cook County is responsible for many of
Western's students, it must also be pointed out that these
people come mainly from the suburban areas about Chicago.
Surprisingly few Chicago students come to Western, although
other urban areas such as Quincy, Rock Island, Moline, Peoria,
and Springfield do contribute large numbers of freshmen and
transfer students. On the other hand, as one would suspect with
the decline in rural population in the Military Tract, Western
is getting fewer and fewer of the sons and daughters of the
farming population of the area.

The scholastic characteristics of Western's students has
likewise changed in the past several years. The great problem in
the past has been that of retention. Over forty-six percent of
the Class of 1965 did not renew their enrollments in the University, and of this number over twenty-three percent were dismissed for scholastic and other reasons. This rigorous standard
set by the University staff had its effects in the following year
when over fifty percent of the Class of 1966 did not return to the
campus.[3]

In the following years the rate of dismissal declined. The
probable reason for this was an ever increasing A.C.T. score for
each succeeding new class. Of the Class of 1971 only seventeen
percent were dismissed, and the non-renewal rate declined to
39.2. By 1968 it was possible for officials of the University to
estimate that about 42.9 percent of the freshmen had been
graduated from the top quarter of their high school classes, and
that almost ninety percent were graduated from the upper half.
About two-thirds of the better applicants—those who were grad-
uating from the top third of their high school classes—were

girls.[4]

College officials are now able to indicate the origins of most of the better students. They do not, as one might assume, come from the suburban areas of Cook County but rather from the larger high schools in the Military Tract. One might well suppose that better northern Illinois students tend to enroll at such institutions as Northwestern, the University of Illinois, or smaller private schools with excellent reputations.

Though high school ranking is important as a factor in securing admittance to Western, the University recognizes the significance of high A.C.T. scores achieved by the individual student. Of those students with low high school rankings admitted in 1968, most if not all were allowed in on the basis of a good A.C.T. score.

From a publication of the Cowles Education Corporation it is possible to compare student entrance statistics of the four schools now under the Board of Governors, as well as Western's standards as related to other schools in the nation. The information compiled in 1967 shows the following comparisons:

1. Western's composite A.C.T. score 23: eighty percent in top half of high school classes.
2. Eastern Illinois University; no composite score given: fifty-eight percent in top two-fifths of high school classes.
3. Illinois Teachers College, Chicago-North; no composite score given: "most" in top one-half of high school classes.
4. Illinois Teachers College, Chicago-South; composite score for men 18.9, for women 18.3: seventy-five percent in top one-half of high school classes. ....
5. Ohio State University; composite score for men 19.7, for women 21.5: seventy-three percent in top one-third of high school classes.
6. Baylor University; composite score for men 24.2, for women 22.8: seventy percent from top one-fourth of high school classes.[5]

IV.

One of President Bernhard's initial projects was the initiation of a five and ten year long range planning program for the University. The second interim report on that program was published in June, 1969, and it represents a significant insight into the possibilities for change at Western Illinois University.

Among the suggested goals for the next decade are:

1. Sharing of research facilities with other senior and junior colleges.
2. Establishment of uniform minimum admission standards "in keeping" with the University's expectations and "with other senior institutions in the state."
3. Extension of graduate education for mid-career professional personnel.
4. Programs of extension and continuing education.
5. More effort on education of disadvantaged youth.
6. Stabilization of lower division enrollments; emphasis on upper division and graduate level work.
7. Increased utilization of physical facilities; increased scheduling of classes in later afternoon and evening hours.*

It is further argued within the general statement attached to the Five and Ten Year Plan that colleges, rather than schools, be formed within the University. According to the Plan a College of Fine Arts has been "sanctioned officially," and that a College of Arts and Sciences should also be created. Further developments should include a College of Communications as well as a School of Nursing.

Some considerable importance is attached to forming a "selective admissions policy" which would admit students who are not only academically qualified, but also students from the "culturally disadvantaged" sections of American society, specially talented persons or veterans who might not otherwise qualify and mature adults without regard to class rank or A.C.T. rank. The University is called upon to develop a remedial program for those students who need "special help," as well as academic counseling for those with less than an adequate background.

*I have taken the liberty to abbreviate wording.

These "high risk" students, as they are called in the Plan, are to be given financial assistance through the waiver of tuition and fees. "A further goal," continued the statement, "would be to provide financial support to cover the cost of books, equipment, housing, and food when such assistance is essential. . . ."

Further goals as stated in the Five and Ten Year Plan include increased or intensified relationships with junior colleges and an enlargement of the graduate program. Doctoral degrees, so says the statement, may be proposed and ready for acceptance by 1979-1980.

It was duly recognized in the Plan that the University's library holdings are pitifully inadequate for any advanced programs at present. Plans are to increase those holdings within a new building to approximately 435,000 volumes by 1974-1975.

A very interesting part of the long range plan of the University treats with the possible expansion of the student enrollment. It is thought that, by 1975, there should be a student population (FTE) of about 18,500, with an instructional staff of 1207. If this occurs, the increase will more than double the size of Western's present student body which totals 9169 (for the year 1968).

A summary of the remainder of the Plan might include the following:

1. The establishment of five vice-presidencies (academic affairs, administration, business affairs, public services, and student affairs).
2. The campus is to remain a ten-minute walking area, with no internal transportation. Murray Street should be relocated.
3. The relocation of Hanson Field.
4. The construction of a new fine arts building.[6]

V.

All of this, to be sure, rests upon the good will of the taxpayer of Illinois. One must remember that the Five and Ten Year Plan only treats with expansion at Western Illinois

University. It does not deal with the intended expansion of facilities at the University of Illinois, the two Chicago state colleges, Southern Illinois University, Eastern Illinois University, Illinois State University, and Northern Illinois University. Surely these institutions will make demands upon the treasury of the state, as will the scores of junior colleges already created or in the making.

What is obvious, however, is that Western Illinois University has come a long way from the thinking of Presidents Henninger and Bayliss. The University could not be recognized today by such men as Professors Drake or Sutherland; nor could it be understood by President Morgan, were he alive today. Perhaps some of these early leaders had the dream; but surely what has happened, what is happening, and what will happen goes beyond the fondest hopes these men may have imagined.

Chapter XI: *A New President For Western*

1. *Vita* on President Bernhard obtained from W.I.U.
2. Copies of two addresses by President Bernhard obtained from W.I.U.
3. Information obtained from Office of Institutional Planning and Development, W.I.U.
4. Interview with officials in Office of Admissions.
5. *How to Pass College Board Admissions Scholastic Aptitude Test* (New York, N.Y.: Cowles Education Corporation, 1967), pp. 422-424, p. 435, p. 416.
6. *Second Interim Progress Report For the Five and Ten Year Long Range Planning Project,* Western Illinois University, 1969.

Bibliography

Interviews:
  Mr. Walter Eller
  Mr. George Gaylor
  Mr. James Grigsby
  Mr. Roy Sallee
  Mr. Kimbrough Shake
  Mr. Rupert Simpkins
  Mrs. Ruth Stocker
  Mr. Wayne Wetzel
  Miss Mary Wyne

Communications or Letters:
  Mr. Harry Anderson
  Miss Wilhelmina Bauch
  Mr. Ralph Bishop
  Mrs. Martha McLean Davis
  Mr. Oliver M. Dickerson
  Mrs. J. B. Glasgow
  Mrs. Goldia Howes
  Mr. Guy Hoyt
  Mrs. Earl Jackson

Collections:
  The James Burns Collection
  The Mrs. J. B. Glasgow Collection
  The Miss Fanny Jackson Collection
  The Presidents' Collection
  The Miss Lauretta Robinson Collection

Unpublished Records:
  Faculty Record: Minutes of First Faculty Meetings.
  Minutes of the Board of Trustees: Western Illinois State Normal School

Institutional Publications:
  Bayliss Memorial Number, 1911, a publication of the *Courier*.
  Faculty Committee Schedule, 1946-1950.
  Faculty Handbook
  Homecoming Bulletin, 1939, 1949.
  Living in Macomb and Teaching at Western Illinois University, n.d.
  The Normal School Quarterly, published during the Morgan era.
  Open Gate and Open Door, 1930.
  Organization Calendar, 1946-1950.
  Reports of President Beu to Teachers College Board
  Seminar Programs, 1904-1905.
  Staff, June 6, 1969.
  Statement of Request For Preliminary Accreditation of the Certificate of Advanced Study in Educational Administration, written for the North Central Association, 1967.

Western Illinois State Teachers College Quarterly, Dec., 1942.
Western Illinois University Charts Its Course

Newspapers and School Periodicals:
  Clionian, a publication of Western Illinois State Normal School.
  Macomb Bystander
  Macomb Journal; referred to in text as Macomb *Journal.*
  The Sequel
  The Westerner, alumni publication of the University.
  The Western Courier, referred to in text as the *Courier.*

Periodicals:
  Bulletin of the American Association of University Professors, Winter, 1960.
  Beu, F. A., "The Teacher's Ethics: A Guide to Successful Professional Rela-
    tions," *Illinois Teacher,* Jan., 1937, pp. 155-158.
  Beu, F. A., "Emotional Maturity and the Teacher," *Illinois Education,* Sept.,
    1942, pp. 5-6, p. 16.
  Grote, Caroline, "The Normal Schools of Illinois," *School News,* July, 1911,
    pp. 512-513.

Other Publications:
  Bateman, Newton and Selby, Paul. *Historical Encyclopedia of Illinois.* Chi-
    cago: Munsell Publishing Co., 1907.
  Hackamack, Lawrence. *An Analysis of the Cost of Attending Western Illinois
    College.* Unpublished thesis, 1948.
  Harper, Charles. *A Century of Public Teacher Education.* Washington, D.C.;
    American Association of Teachers Colleges, 1939.
  How to Pass College Board Admissions Scholastic Aptitude Test. New York,
    N.Y.: Cowles Education Corporation, 1967.
  Plochmann, George K. *The Ordeal of Southern Illinois University.* Carbon-
    dale, Ill.: Southern Illinois Press, n.d.
  Proceedings of the Illinois State Teachers Association. Springfield: n.d.
  Proceedings of the Teachers College Board. Springfield: 1918-1935.
  Schlesinger, Arthur. *The Rise of the City, 1878-1898.* New York, N.Y.: Mac-
    millan, 1933.

Speeches:
  Address to the Class of 1972, Sept. 4, 1968, President John T. Bernhard.
  Address to the Faculty, Sept. 11, 1968, President John T. Bernhard.
  "The Crisis in Our Culture," President A. L. Knoblauch, published by West-
    ern Illinois University Press, 1968.

Administrative Reports and Interviews:
  Information and Data, collected by the Office of Institutional Planning and
    Development.
  Interviews in Office of Admissions, Western Illinois University.
  *Second Interim Progress Report For Five and Ten Year Long Range Planning
    Report,* printed by Central Administration, Western Illinois University,
    1969.

Index